SHOTGUNNER'S NOTEBOOK

SHOTGUNNER'S NOTEBOOK

The Advice and Reflections of a Wingshooter

by
GENE HILL

Illustrations by Fred Rothenbush

COUNTRYSPORT PRESS
Traverse City, Michigan

Printed in the United States of America

Library of Congress Catalog Card Number: 89-060724

ISBN 0-924357-00-2

Dedication

I would be a lot less than honest if I ascribed much of this book as my own deep thinking, research, and experimentation. Rather, it has been the result of knowing and reading and spending time and shooting with so many truly knowledgeable people whom I've been privileged to call "friend."

So I gratefully thank Cyril Adams, Bob Brister, Jim Carmichael, Dick Dietz, Rudy Etchen, Grits Gresham, Jay Herbert, Mike McIntosh, Billy Perdue, Steve Smith, John Wooters, and Don Zutz – among the host of others who were kind and patient enough to hear me out and answer my questions with quiet civility – which I'm sure wasn't always that easy.

Contents

About The Artist

Fred Rothenbush of Ruskin, Florida is one of this country's most outstanding sporting artists. He is also a gifted portrait painter, having executed works for Presidents Dwight D. Eisenhower, John F. Kennedy, and Ronald Regan.

Fred is also an accomplished wingshooter and dog man, and regularly shoots at some of the better plantations across his native South.

His pencil studies were commissioned especially for this book.

Introduction

Let me say at first that this book is meant to help, make you question, disagree if you wish and, now and then, amuse; hopefully it will do all of these.

There is little here of inches and pounds. I leave that to the many who do it far better than I. All I offer is a series of suggestions, theories, a few prejudices, and the occasional fact.

We know that the shotgun really has not been changed much in close to a hundred years. This and that have been moved here and there, our shells are better, and the ancillary gadgetry has gone forth and multiplied to where the mind is truly staggered, but the essentials have remained traditional.

We enjoy and study and argue the minutia but, at bottom, our shotguns are to the wingshooter as the brush is to the artist, a tool to help make the portrait of a day of sport both memorable and satisfying; without it the possessing of game would be merely barbaric.

I consider this book to be interesting but not <u>important</u>. I am no Greener or Burrard. I offer nothing new or revolutionary, rather a warm return to familiar – reminders that in the hands and minds of many men the shotgun was intended to be a work of art, and they made them that way – for both functional and spiritual reasons. The beauty of the fine shotgun can be easily interpreted as an homage – to the game, to the concept of true sport, and the ethics of the hunt that, hopefully, will be primary in our usage and appreciation.

Lastly, I'd like to thank the good folks at Gun Dog magazine who published many of these Notebook entries over the years. Your support is appreciated.

Fred Rothenbush

THE
GUNS

Our World Without Shotguns

As a man unfortunate enough to have to plod shamefully through life without a nice side-by-side 28 gauge, or even a decent boxlock 12 (28-inch barrels, straight grip, bored improved cylinder and modified), I have long periods of time when I feel a little sorry for myself. It was one of these low periods when I was wishing I had a little more money or a little more common sense (asking for both would be too much) that I began wondering what our world would be like if there weren't any shotguns at all.

I doubt if we'd have any Labradors, goldens, Brittanies, springers, setters, pointers, shorthairs, or beagles if there were no shotguns.

We wouldn't have field trials, duck clubs, or all those nifty-looking pins for our hats. We wouldn't collect shooting sticks, shell bags, tweed hats, leather boots, duck calls, or flasks if there weren't shotguns.

Without shotguns, there wouldn't be any skeet (I wouldn't

miss high 5, though), trap, quail walks, wipe-your-eye, high tower, or pasture afternoons with a hand trap.

We'd never know the joy of fried rabbit, honey-glazed mallard, fricasseed squirrel with dumplings, roast goose, fried quail, broiled dove, or pheasant with sauerkraut and sausage if it weren't for the shotgun.

There wouldn't be any Hennessey duck marshes, Reneson grouse covers, Maass canvasbacks, or Ripley woodcock if they didn't have shotguns.

Would we have L. L. Bean, Orvis, Gokey, Dunn's, or Woolrich? I doubt it. We wouldn't have the neighborhood sports shop to hang around in and gab, much less Wild Wings, Crossroads of Sport, Collectors Covey, Sportsman's Edge, and the others who have the carvings and sculpture and the art that all came about just because of the shotgun.

There wouldn't be any thick coffee cups with wood ducks or puppies on them. No camouflage neckties, red flannel shirts, shooting vests, or heavy parkas. Easton, Maryland; Grand Junction, Tennessee; Vandalia, Ohio; or Stuttgart, Arkansas, would each be just another small American town.

None of these names would mean anything to you either: Nash Buckingham, Burton Spiller, Corey Ford, Havilah Babcock, Ed Zern, Robert Ruark, Archibald Rutledge, Eugene Connett, Dave Newell, or John Alden Knight. And Samson, Reiger, McManus, Trueblood, Barrett, and Brister would likely be names on a factory timecard.

Whose pulse would quicken at the morning call of <u>bob white</u>, <u>bob white</u>, or the evening song of geese or the chatter of mallards? The pheasant, chukar, wild turkey, and a host of others would just be pictures in dusty books.

There wouldn't be any reason to get up and have a diner breakfast with your buddies at 4 a.m. Or learn to make sandwiches two inches thick, or carry an extra candy bar. We wouldn't dream about sink boxes, Barnegat Bay scullers, or layout blinds. Or find any delight in a November northeast wind. I know I'd miss the arguments about 3-inch magnums, 2's versus 4's, and the virtues of copper over lead. I wouldn't own six pairs of long johns, wouldn't care about not being able to find my handwarmers or whatever happened to my sheepskin mittens. I'd probably have a car in my garage instead of piles of decoys and an olive-drab boat. And I wouldn't have a hole in my rug, a chewed-up chair, and three ruined pairs of shoes either, because I wouldn't have Maggie.

I'd never have spent any time looking for abandoned farm orchards, alder swamps, or spring-run pastures. There wouldn't be any old collars and dog bells in the barn, and I'd have no reason to turn my head and blow my nose if someone started to talk about Little Ben, Daisy, Belle, Rocky, or Tip. My suits wouldn't be all covered with dog hair, my car seats wouldn't be muddy and torn, and there wouldn't be a special stone or tree here and there in my lawn. I'd never have had the sun in my eyes, my pants hung up on barbed wire, or the safety on. Sixes, 7½'s, and 8's might only mean hat sizes.

Who would have thought of building a hollow-cedar Canada, making a root-head swan, or a sleeping black duck? Why bother with carving a dainty, slender wooden yellowlegs or turnstone? How much poorer we would have been without the likes of the Wards, Elmer Crowell, Shang Wheeler, or Ira Jester. What would be magic about the Susquahanna Flats or Merrymeeting Bay or Tule Lake?

Fred Kimble, Doc Carver, Adam Bogardus, Annie Oakley, or Rudy Etchen might have taken up golf.

A hundred thousand Englishmen and Scots would be playing cricket, or worse, tennis, on the twelfth of August.

Opening day wouldn't have any special meaning except for worm fishermen and baseball fans. Oliver Winchester would be famous for sewing machines, Remington for the typewriter, and the brothers Parker for coffee grinders. I might have a car less than seven years old if it weren't for Lefever, Baker, Smith, Greener, Hussey, etc., etc., and just possibly a savings account.

I wouldn't have a dozen coats that are fit only for duck blinds or briars and only a couple for weddings and funerals. I wouldn't have eight pairs of boots and only two pairs of good shoes – one brown, one black. Ninety-five percent of my neckties wouldn't have birds or dogs (or chili) on them. And most of my vests, hats, and raingear wouldn't be camouflage.

No shotguns, no poetry. No shotguns, no exuberant competition. No shotguns, no silent days alone, or with a dog, to merely walk and think. Take the shotguns from my life and take the books that go with them. Take the paintings and the etchings and bronzed pointing setters and Labs with a proudly carried duck. Take my decoys and my marsh boat and my string of calls. Take my old photographs of friends at gun clubs and duck camps and at the simple farms. Take my faded coats and briared boots and old soft hats. Take my whistles and dog bells and red and yellow field trial ribbons from their frames.

What friends I have, what days I treasure most, what places that I think about and smile...they are because shotguns are. Without them I would have been empty. They have made my life full.

Nothing that I have is worth a lot, and yet nothing that I have is so priceless. The treasures are not the guns themselves, but behind the doors that they open.

As I write this I'm thinking about tomorrow. Toward late afternoon I'll take a gun and a dog and walk an hour, not caring all that much about the chances for a pheasant or an evening duck, but satisfied to have the heft of half a dozen shells and to watch the puppy lark around a little. Behind the yellow lights of home are the voices from the pictures and books that never ask, "Did you get anything?" but always ask, "Did you have a good time?" And as I put the shotgun back in its corner I can always answer, "Yes."

Appreciation

I'm afraid I have to plead guilty – at least privately – to the sin of covetousness when it comes to shotguns. I say that since my experience in this arena leads me to believe that out of a random group of say, a thousand shotgunners, at least 999 are right there drooling with me.

The imaginary shotgunner that I like to talk to – or write to – is a dreamer of sorts. He has a fine appreciation for the intricate artistry that results in a fine gun not only being aesthetically rewarding, but so intricately and ingeniously crafted that it functions as instinctively in his hands as if it were part of him. He will appreciate the totality of the creation – from the grain of the wood to the sweep of the rib – with the same feeling of marvel and with the same valid reasons that might hold him for some time contemplating a fine painting or sculpture, or the complexities of architecture, or even those unanswerable questions we ask of no one in particular when we hold a grouse or pintail in our hands.

Few things in this world so marvelously combine form and function as a good, or even not so good, shotgun, and to forget this and its ramifications, both mechanical and artistic, is to deny ourselves many of the great satisfactions that owning a gun or appreciating a particular one affords.

More than a few of us shoot and hunt according to the philosophy that form and function count. I don't see much to fault with falling in love with a rich and beautiful woman – or at least admiring one even if you can't have her. I see little harm in permitting myself an idle dream of my retriever being less of a skylark than she is, or my long wanted English gun being a best-grade sidelock, or suddenly coming into an unsuspected inheritance.

There's no point in shutting your mind to the fact that these delightful things do exist and, in my opinion, taking a little time to prattle about them doesn't hurt. Where would a minister be without the help of sin, or the dry without alcohol?

Locks

Every once in a while someone who doesn't know better asks me to help them out with their shooting. I tell them that I believe the best shooting coach is a case of shells – right after they've learned the basics of foot position and gun mounting.

But there's one piece of advice that is worth repeating again and again, and that is to keep moving the gun and follow the target or bird after it is missed. This is the way to correct yourself; by staying with the target, you'll find out if you were behind or over or lifting your head from the stock. You'll be surprised how easy it is to do once the noise and furor are over and you're in your quiet moment of humbleness.

All this was brought home to me on a recent dove shoot in Mexico. I was having a bad time of it overall. I'd take three or four straight doves and then miss the same number of identical shots – but by staying with the gun, I discovered that I was "checking" or stopping my swing ever so briefly, but enough to shoot behind.

The fault wasn't in my technique, for once, but in the trigger pulls of the gun I had borrowed – they were about a pound more than I can handle with consistency. Once I was satisfied with this, I managed to switch guns (to a lovely old side-lever hammer Boss), and I began to do better. I still missed a lot more than I should have, but I don't know but one or two dove hunters who wouldn't say the same thing.

The old theory about trigger pulls is that they should be half the weight of the gun; a seven-pound gun ought to have a trigger set at 3½ pounds. If it's a double trigger, the second one is traditionally a half-pound heavier.

But everyone is different – or almost everyone. I like triggers that are very crisp with almost no discernible creep, and I like them no heavier than three pounds unless the gun is a brute running nine or so pounds, like some of the old 32-inch barreled side-by-side, 3-inch magnums.

In general, I believe that by holding the forward hand a bit short, we can accommodate a longish stock and vice-versa, but if the triggers are too light or too heavy, we are about to have a rather bad day. Many of our modern production guns have very heavy triggers pulls, some because the makers won't spend the time to check and refine them, and others because of the legal problems that might arise with a gun whose triggers were set too light.

If you've been having one of those mysterious problems where everything "looks good" but nothing falls or breaks, check the triggers for pull weight and smoothness. Once you get everything set where you like it, don't think they won't change; they can by being over-dry or over-oiled or by a piece of grit, or just by getting old or not being all that well made in the first place.

Certain guns were famous for finely adjusted triggers – the Model 21 Winchester was one, and oddly enough I have good trigger pulls on both my Remington 870 and my 1100. My old Winchester Model 97 pump is a horror to keep right; maybe it's just old and cranky or just plain tired. I've had some "best quality" English sidelock guns with unreliable pulls as well, but this sort of gun is ordinarily capable of being adjusted to perfection.

23

You would think that any gunsmith could work on a trigger, but that's not the case. I've seen some very bad work from some so-called "trigger specialists," especially in the release triggers I use in my competition guns. The only advice I can give you is to ask around or have the gunsmith give you some sort of assurance that he will work on your gun again if the pulls aren't right and reduce his charges accordingly. Usually, a good professional cleaning can put a trigger back where it belongs. A year-long residue of oil can gum up the works like tar. The triggers of an old Merkel I was fond of but didn't use for a year or two for various reasons looked like they had been dipped in varnish when my gunsmith took it apart; once cleaned, they were as good as new.

It's good to remember that in very cold weather, any trigger ought to be cleaned of all oil or grease and the firing pin passages cleaned as well. One drop of oil can turn the whole thing to stone when the temperature gets around zero. I admit to being reminded of this the hard way when I borrowed an old side-by-side from a farmer friend and spent a week with a gun with an inoperable left barrel. I knew quickly what the problem was, but didn't want to take the gun apart and hoped that an evening or two by the stove would work – but it didn't. I was only a young boy then and wouldn't have the same hesitation now, providing I had the use of a perfectly fitting screwdriver...which is something I carry with all my good guns, hoping to never have to use it. Good old Hoppes and an old toothbrush will do the job, but be sure to wipe everything dry when you're done.

I think that most gunsmiths would agree that all of us over-oil our guns all the time; use the spray can of stuff only on the outside and a dropper or toothpick with one drop here and there on the inside. A few minutes with your gunsmith learning where and how to oil your guns is a very smart investment. Gunmakers ought to include such advice but, perhaps wisely, they don't encourage the likes of me to go too deeply into gun repair or maintenance.

A small but interesting point is that if you have a light trigger, you will get greater control of the movement by pulling with the tip pad of your finger; if the pull is heavy, move the control down to the crease of the first joint. I've known some trapshooters who pull the trigger by using the base of the trigger finger, right down by the palm, and firing by clenching the whole hand. This is done with the hopes of easing a flinch; it didn't work with me and felt terribly awkward and imprecise as well.

A bad or overly powerful trigger pull can affect your shooting by putting too much force into the trigger hand – this can come about as a bad habit induced by heavy-pulling triggers to start with. If your whole trigger system and your handling of it is smooth and "automatic," one of the more mysterious causes of missing will be absent – at least for a while.

It's not a bad idea to save a few empty shells to use for letting down the hammers, or use snap caps. I don't like to pull the triggers on an empty chamber – it's a bad and dangerous habit. It's really not at all necessary to put a gun away with the "hammers down." I never bother with it myself, but if you're going to test trigger pulls, you'll need something for resistance against the firing pins.

I'm surprised that so many gun writers rather dismiss the importance of the shotgun trigger; not only the force of pull, but even its placement in the trigger guard is of some importance, for even a subliminal annoyance can build into an annoyance that will cause uneven performance on the part of the gunner.

Another case in point is that I was having trouble with

a good side-by-side that I shot a lot but always felt "uncomfortable" with in spite of shooting it fairly well. A genius of a gunsmith, no longer with us, moved the trigger back about one-quarter of an inch and that solved my unconscious groping, smoothed out the handling, and gave the gun that mysterious sweetness of feel we are always searching for.

Stocks

L̷ast fall I was in England (luckily enough) shooting driven pheasant with some rather good shots. Being Americans, they favored the use of over-unders, not out of prejudice, but because these are the guns they shoot at home.

Unfortunately, one of the over-unders broke on the very first day and the only replacement was a side-by-side owned by the man running our shoot. The unlucky shooter is a short man, one who for years has used a stock about 13 inches long, and the borrowed gun, a fine grade sidelock, was 14½ inches long and much straighter at the comb than our friend was used to using. He muttered about the probability of not being able to even mount the gun, much less being able to hit the rather difficult high crossing and incoming birds we had to cope with, but it was either try to make it work or become a spectator.

I was on the stand next to him during the first drive when he used the "new" gun. To be honest, he hadn't been shooting all that well with his own gun, and I was worried that his whole trip would be ruined with a gun he obviously didn't feel enthusiastic about in the first place.

As luck would have it, the birds virtually poured over his stand – and he shot better than I'd ever seen him do before. After the day was over we sat down and discussed how this could have happened. What was the magic in a gun that he would have summarily rejected if there had been the least opportunity?

It seemed to me, as we sat in the gun room while he practiced mounting the borrowed gun, that the added length forced him to bring the gun to his face, and the decreased drop at comb kept his face where it belonged on the stock; the combination of the two also moved his hand position where he was a bit freer or quicker in moving the gun.

I realize that this sounds like a lot to digest out of one sentence, but it is the essence of the English theory – I'd better say the essence of an English theory – of the efficiency of longer and straighter stocks. If you go back in time, say 50 years or more, and compare the dimensions of the average, not custom-fitted, stock of the British guns and the American ones, you'd immediately notice the difference. Ours have more drop at both heel and comb, and the stocks are often a bit thicker and, in general, shorter. Whether this is the legacy, as is the omnipresent pistol grip, of being a "nation of riflemen," I'm not sure, but it seems at least likely.

Unfortunately, nothing seems to have changed all that much. The average American factory stock is still too thick, has too much curve in the pistol grip, and has too much drop and pitch – at least for my taste in a field gun.

While no blanket statement is worth defending to your last breath – especially when it comes to something as individual or whimsical as a shotgun – I really believe that most of us would shoot better with a stock a bit longer and a bit straighter. The other nuances of the typical English stock are a bit of cast-off for the right-handed shooter and a bit of toe out, both of which can add a good deal to the comfort of shooting as well as quickness and accuracy. I believe that the average American field stock makes us shoot low and that the oft-cited tendency to lift our heads is, at bottom, a rather natural urge to see what we're shooting at instead of peering at our thumb or the back of the receiver.

One other factor – again, in my opinion – is that our friend in England had put away a gun that weighed about eight pounds or a shade more in exchange for the borrowed gun that was a full pound lighter. Many authorities feel that the 12 gauge field gun that weighs more than seven to 7½ pounds is greatly inhibiting to necessary quick mounting and swinging.

We often talk about "smoothness" of swing, but in reality that's not quite the case. The upland bird hunter most often has to deal with a target that is a lot more erratically zigging and zagging than going off on a single plane of flight, and he has to be able to be a gun <u>pointer</u> – regardless of all the talk about swing.

The pistol grip is made to use as a fulcrum. A right-handed shooter will swing his gun more with the right hand than with the hand holding the barrels. While this is fine for target shooting, it does tend to inhibit field shooting a bit. The English, or straight-hand, grip forces us to use both hands more and can give us more barrel control on a wildly changing target. No doubt this is also subject to argument, but the facts are the facts. I think my friend with the borrowed side-by-side was able to shoot not only faster with the lighter gun, but was able to better control the barrels, whether consciously or subconsciously. The theory here is that the closer the hands are in line with the barrels, as with the straight-grip, the more responsive the gun – the more "alive" it feels.

In general, there's no better or more sure way to improve the average field gun than to do what you can to improve the stock. While this sort of gunsmithing is beyond the capabilities of most of us, it isn't all that expensive to have the pistol grip curve lessened to a quarter or half pistol or removed altogether. Nor is it all that difficult on most pumps or autos to have the stock refitted by bending the stock bolt a bit and putting shims at the receiver end to make it a bit straighter at the comb. I don't know as I would do all this much alteration on a gun that was used primarily or exclusively for waterfowl, but if I did a great deal of upland gunning or dove shooting with a particular gun, I would give it some thought. You might borrow a gun with a straight-hand grip and see if it felt better to you. As for lengthening the stock, that's just a matter of some shims behind the buttplate, but you have to stick with it a bit to get the new feel.

I've always believed that the really infinite measurements that you might end up with using a try-stock for a guide aren't all that critical. Most of us can and do shoot respectably with a bit of doctoring. If we get into one of those deep slumps or are just uncomfortable with a gun, there's no harm in a bit of experimentation. A stock should fit as well as possible – finances and all that being considered – but there are a lot of shooters using stocks that are so far out of line with their builds as to make any success they might have purely coincidental.

The bottom line is common sense. I would prefer, given the choice, to have my guns well stocked with fine wood rather than covered with engraving. I'd rather look good shooting than have what I'm shooting look good!

Those of you who have as much respect as I do for the great John M. Browning will remember the superb dimensions of his stocks – and the small pistol grip as well as the choice of having no pistol grip at all. I don't know of any of the old Browning designs that weren't great "pointers," and his stock dimensions and configurations were no small part of it. Why such ideas have fallen into disfavor is one of the mysteries of our time.

In case you think that this little discussion has to do only with doubles, I didn't mean it that way. Gun handling facility is the same regardless of the action. The Brownings I just referred to are the old autos and pumps. The old Winchester Model 12 at one time had the option of a straight stock – and that's what I used for quite a while shooting trap. I believe that the old Model 31 Remington pump was also offered with such a stock. I certainly wish the new ones were, along with a couple of other options such as length of pull and a bit of cast, but it's not about to be.

Barrels (and Balance)

There is a growing trend (maybe a conspiracy!) among today's gunmakers to afflict us with gun barrels that, to me, are on the short side. Commonly, if you want a gun bored improved cylinder and modified, you find that you have to take 26-inch barrels; if you want 28-inch barrels, the gun will likely be bored modified and full. Why? Because it's easy for the maker to do it that way – call it the Detroit Syndrome.

Perversely, it's just the gun that <u>needs</u> a longer barrel that only comes with the short one – the typical 20 gauge, which I'd like to see offered in 28 inch and with the option of a 30.

I don't know where it got started, but this goes back to the misbegotten concept of the "brush gun." Maybe it was borrowed from the rifle makers and the development of the carbine and saddle gun, but it ought to have occurred to some designer that a rifle is shot when it is held still and a shotgun is shot when it is (hopefully) moving. They talk about <u>quickness</u> when the more desirable factor is <u>smoothness</u>. Moments of inertia, the feel of a shotgun, the qualities that make a shotgun a fluid, continually moving instrument, are the desirable factors. And while speed is nice, it is not in itself the great be-all and end-all that many makers would have us believe.

Barrel length is both a question of esthetics and function; esthetically a lot depends on the size of the shooter. A 20 gauge with 26-inch barrels can be very fitting in the hands of a youngster or a lady, and totally inappropriate in the hands of a man six feet tall. The great Brothers Purdey liked to build their 20 and 28 gauges with 28- and 30-inch barrels – and correctly so. The diminutive size of a small bore needs length for the eye as well as the hand. It is the overall weight of a gun, its balance, and its ease of handling that are critical to good shooting, and short barrels enhance none of these.

In a 12-gauge gun, whose proper weight for field use ought to be no more than seven pounds, a 27-inch barrel is as short as I'd shoot, and I would much prefer 28, 29, or even 30. Why? They simply handle better. I prefer to be sure rather than fast; I'd rather swing through than poke, and I want a barrel length that almost insists that I do, rather than one that I have to coax.

There is little question that our top skeet shooters, in order to get and stay with their 99+ averages, have to pay more than a little attention to every detail of their guns. What barrel lengths are they shooting? Twenty-eight inches. Those that use the ubiquitous Remington 1100 with a 26-inch barrel have the added weight and balance of several inches of receiver to achieve the same fluid start and follow-through. Most AA trapshooters will shoot a barrel as long as they can handle, as likely a 32-inch over-under, and a single barrel of equal or longer length is routine. A gun that's too easy to start is also too easy to stop. Or put another way, "there's no such thing as a free lunch."

The current leaning toward short-barreled guns is a result of a need to reduce overall weight. The mass-produced gun of today cannot hope to offer the balance and "aliveness" of the incredibly expensive "best" guns of the past. The modern gun builder knows that the customer is going to complain if he's hurt by recoil, so he builds a 7½-pound gun and shortens the barrels and says the gun is fast-handling. Well, it may look that way, and it may even feel that way when you're carrying it, but the bottom line is how you perform when you're <u>shooting</u>.

The most famous move toward short barrels was the brainchild of Robert Churchill, his notorious XXV – the 25-inch barrel he introduced about 60 years ago. The traditionalists argued that it didn't look right, that it would lessen velocity, that it would make you check your swing. Churchill said that all was nonsense and ended up with a fair-sized following using either one of his guns or a copy following what seemed then a strong trend. Of course, Churchill was right about velocity and patterns. Barrel length has a negligible effect on either, and he insisted that faster was better and a lot of shooters believed him. No doubt a lot of them did shoot better with a XXV, but probably because of the fine balance of the Churchill – or that mysterious faith that makes any of us a believer when we're convinced that we've gone and done the right thing. If faith can move mountains, it can certainly handle the XXV! But the fad didn't persevere, and the trend in British shooting is back to longer barrels. In today's markets, my argument for longer barrels has to settle itself on the small-bore shotguns. You just can't get a 12 bore, 28-inch barreled gun that weighs less than seven pounds that I know of unless you are willing to spend the kind of money that will buy a measure of hand craftsmanship. But they are available, most of them imported from Spain and Italy.

I own and shoot a Greener with original 24-inch barrels. And while I love the little gun, I certainly can't brag on my success with it. When I shot it exclusively and kept constant, conscious awareness of its quickness and forced myself to try to follow through, I did a fair job with it. But I never shot it as well as I do either of my 28-inch barreled guns – including a current love in 28 gauge.

Of course the niceties of balance, that of having the total control of the gun between the hands, is not in itself a function of barrel length or weight, but of design – or genius. My point is, simply, that given a choice of a nicely balanced gun, with the same weight, I would figure on shooting better with the one with the longer barrels. My eye would be more "conscious" of where the barrels were pointing, and my hands would more easily perform the desirable follow-through.

I have a Perazzi that I use almost exclusively for my live-pigeon shooting. It has two sets of barrels, one 29 inches, the other 31 inches, and both weigh the same. Which do I do better with? The longer ones, although how much better, I can't say. I feel that the swing is less choppy and more positive and, while not as quick, certainly quick enough in a game where speed is very essential. A lot of live-bird shooters will disagree – but that's the nature of shooters, and I hope that such questioning and discussion never ends.

I'll end this with a quote from the great English gun writer/engineer, Gough Thomas: "I have no doubt that the current popularity of the shorter-barreled gun springs from an intuitive appreciation of these things, particularly on the part of shooters who are no longer prodigal of their energy...But it should not be necessary to cut barrels down to twenty-five inches to attain the balance standards of the past. The danger is that if shooters do not appreciate and demand well-balanced guns, the trade will not bother to produce them."

To which I say Amen!

Over-Unders
or
Side-by-Sides?

Which "points" better, the side-by-side or the over-under? This intriguing question is among the oldest bandied about by shotgunners. The argument is the usual mixture of prejudice, fact, and wishful thinking – a delightful broth!

The standard British argument – pro side-by-side, of course – is that, although the over-under preceded the side-by-side, the latter became the gun of choice in a land of devout wingshooters because it performed better. By the way, in Britain it's: "under-over."

The other side, mostly American, says that the side-by-side is a relic, surviving out of sentiment and stubbornness. Most adherents will add, "Put them up against each other in the hands of comparable shooters, and the over-under will always win!"

Neither argument is absolutely true.

The over-under was the predecessor of the side-by-side, but many reasons gave the side-by-side the early edge. Basic among them are that the side-by-side is (or was) easier to load in the confines of a shooting butt and built with less overall weight. But the bottom line has to be this: The success of the side-by-side must be laid to the fact that sportsmen felt they could score better with it.

Today, almost all the same statements can be made, with the exception of ease in loading, about the over-under. The gracefulness is a matter of taste, but I believe that most of us would still give that nod to the side-by-side because of its sleek, low profile. Yet, that's a matter of taste, for as much as I admire these classic lines, I was recently shooting a 16 bore over-under Boss that was as handsome a gun as I've ever held. In looks, we'd better call it a draw.

One of the common arguments is that recoil is usually felt less in the over-under than the side-by-side. Again, this is a matter of stock dimension, weight, and a dash of prejudice. It's true that while the over-under barrels tend to move less and do so in a vertical plane (given equivalent weight in components, barrels, etc.) and the side-by-side moves a bit more in the direction of the barrel being fired, neither is really vital in a shooting situation and the effects are as imagined as they are real.

One effect that is real is the wind resistance of the over-under, as those of you who have shot trap or skeet with one on a breezy day can testify. This, again, is something most of us can live with and I'd relegate it to "hairsplitting."

What the arguments are really about is this: Which gun will produce the better score? It's almost impossible today to make much of a competition case for the side-by-side. I used to shoot with a few top gunners who shot Model 21 Winchesters. I did myself for a few years, but I doubt if a shooter who has any serious intentions of winning a trophy in tight competition would choose a side-by-side in clay target competition. Why? I really can't answer. I don't think anyone could drag out a list of facts and add them up and say, "This is why." I suspect it's largely a matter of the ready availability of inexpensive over-unders, largely the superb Brownings in the period after the second World War when target shooting grew by leaps and bounds; we got used to using the over-unders.

Another common theory is that we are a nation of riflemen (but I'm not one) and most of us started shotgunning with a pump gun, hence the gravitation to the single sighting plane. I shot a Model 12 Winchester when I started competitive trap, as did almost everyone else, then went to the Model 21 for reasons I don't remember but shot it about as well as the Model 12, and I finally ended up with a Krieghoff. There were very few "target" side-by-sides made, with the exception of the live-pigeons guns which we'll come to in a minute. Parker was a contributor, L.C. Smith, Fox, and Ithaca as well, but in a rather limited way – essentially the target guns, aside from the single barrels, were heavier bird guns with hand-filling beavertail forends and higher ribs. A lot of shooters shot them well, and I suspect that most of our top shooters could handle a side-by-side with some distinction if they put their minds to it.

There are enough theories about the merits of the two guns to fill this book, but they are theories – pattern elevation is claimed as a plus for the trapshooter's over-under, skeet shooters like the "lightened" recoil, and on and on. But the bottom line is they paid their money and they took their choice: the over-under.

In the world circuit of live-pigeon shooting, the picture is a bit different. As I've said before, I think this is the most difficult, by far, of all smoothbore shooting. For the most part, the sport is dominated by Europeans, mainly the Italians. Their favorite gun? Usually a double-trigger side-by-side. They say this is a faster gun, quicker to the mark, and I believe it is. Pigeon shooting is more concerned with vertical leads than clay targets, and the Italians like the swiftness of the double gun on a darting, climbing bird.

Is a side-by-side really quicker than an over-under? How would you prove it? Of course, most pigeon shooters shoot an over-under, cost being a factor in guns of this quality as well as the prejudice and conviction that every shooter carries.

The most valid arguments in favor of either type are slightly contradictory. The preference for the over-under in competitive shooting (remember the remarks on live-pigeon shooting) is the idea of visual precision. They say it is easier for the eye to align a narrow plane against the sort of background where we shoot targets than it is a broad plane. Regardless of the experiments with a high rib on the side-by-side, the eye is still conscious of both barrels.

The advantage of the broad, eye-catching expanse of side-by-side barrels is assumed to be in the field, with its variety of backgrounds and vagaries of light.

My controversial conclusion? When the target is a relative constant (you know almost precisely where it will appear and when), the single, narrow sighting plane of the over-under is an advantage to precision alignment. When the target is "random" and some <u>exactness</u> must be sacrificed for <u>speed</u>, then the side-by-side has the advantage.

I also believe that as a field gun the side-by-side has a few other pluses. It is easier to carry – more comfortable over the arm or with the barrels carried over the shoulder; it generally has a better <u>line</u>, the hands are more parallel, especially with a straight or English-style stock, and the tendency to "track" or be <u>too</u> precise is reduced. This last point is somewhat critical to the gunner who says that he simply cannot shoot as well with a side-by-side.

Here I say that too many field shooters are too barrel conscious. The really top-rank gunner is barely aware of his gun barrels; he sees "through" them and his eye is <u>always</u> focused on the target, <u>never</u> down the rib of the shotgun. Why do I say that? The magnificent Italian gunners often shoot a live-pigeon gun whose stock is so high that it is virtually impossible to see the barrels at all; they are "shooting over the end of the gun." I know too well that old habits die hard and shooting styles can be so ingrained that they cannot be changed. I certainly have a few habits that I wish I could toss overboard!

My own shooting generally follows this pattern: over-unders for competition and the side-by-side for the field. Furthermore, I shoot an over-under in the live pigeon ring but believe I might do a little better with a side-by-side except for the fact that I prefer a release trigger here, and the complication of fitting them to a side-by-side double barrel has stymied me. But I would like to at least try one someday to test my theories.

When all is said and done, I doubt if the score at the end of a year in the field would be all that different. That's fine since we don't, and shouldn't, keep this at a competitive level. One of the great pleasures of owning a shotgun is our appreciation of its esthetics – regardless of how the barrels are fastened together. One of my friends, a nationally known skeet champion, favors an old Parker side-by-side with which he has won more than a few prestigious tournaments. He admits to being a "dinosaur," but explains, with a slight smile, that he "would rather turn in a 198 with the Parker than a 200 with anything else." Such is the world of the shotgunner and I, for one, hope the arguments, the debates, and the hairsplitting never, ever cease.

The
Right
Choke

Not too long ago, I was lucky enough to be gunning in Florida on an old-time quail plantation. The dogs were superb, and I even partook of a little duck shooting at the end of the day to round off a most pleasant experience. The only problem was me.

For the past few years, common enough for a long-time shooter, my hearing has deteriorated. When the wind blows and the birds are a little spooky and not lying tight to the dog, I find that I just don't hear them flush and have to rely on what I can see. The same thing holds true in the duck blind – I don't often hear the whistling wings of the approaching duck; I have to rely on my field of vision. More than one flock has passed over me only to be seen as it moved swiftly out of range. Most of the time I can hear the booming flush of a ruffed grouse, or a cock pheasant if he cackles on takeoff. The relatively soft rise of a woodcock often goes unheard.

Well, what can we do about a loss of hearing? First, grin and bear it. I find that wearing a hearing aid in the woods is worse than not hearing. The sound of the shotgun is very unpleasant and the noise of wind and crackling brush underfoot becomes disturbing. The solution is to rely on our eyes and common bird sense – and re-examine our thinking about perfect chokes.

As we get older, we get slower. Even a little bit of that ought to merit some thinking out. First off, most of my field shooting is now done with a 12-gauge gun. The greater pattern efficiency of the larger bore means fewer misses or – more important – fewer crippled birds. You can take my word for it or do some test patterning yourself: A one-ounce load in a 12-gauge gun will have more consistent pattern density than a one-ounce load in a 20 gauge. We'll get into more detail in a minute.

If you take the normal quail shot, one in the relatively open "piney woods" type of cover, the first shot will be about 20 yards and the second another five to 10 yards for a shooter with average reflexes and timing. What I've done is add another five yards to both of these figures, which is about the jump a bird will get on me when I don't hear it well enough to be looking in the right place every time.

The basis for my theory, for any bird hunting including waterfowl, is that we must be prepared for borderline situations. If we're duck hunting and everything pitches down into the decoys, the average shot is about 25 or 30 yards. If we're there with a full-choke autoloader, common sense says that we now have a pleasant margin of time and distance to make sure of our shooting. We don't have to rush because we know that our gun is very effective out to 40 or 45 yards – nothing wrong with that, is there? In the upland bird field the same thing applies, except that heavy cover is going to cost us a shot now and then. But no one promised us a rose garden, or good hearing, in the first place.

What chokes should we use, then, for quail or grouse or woodcock? My current favorite gun is a 12-bore side-by-side that has choke tubes installed. I'll put in improved cylinder for the first barrel and improved modified or full for the second. When I use the same gun on ducks, which I often do, I go to a modified tube in the first barrel, or if everything is spooky and "on the fringe," resume using full and full.

The whole concept of shotgunning, although rather complex in its variations and possibilities, is based on "margin of error." The tighter chokes that I use now give me the same function at 35 yards as the more open ones gave me at 25. I am trading time for distance. Not that I'm a legend with my old boxlock side-by-side, but I've found that the game bag isn't that much lighter and often I do better because subconsciously I <u>know</u> I have extra time. Where a really wild day in the quail field upsets the skeet & skeet gunner because his effective choking is designed for the 25 to 30-yard shot, we aren't troubled.

It is unfortunate that virtually all our domestic 20 gauges are about the same weight as the British or European 12; the theoretical trade-off of effectiveness for quickness and light weight doesn't apply. So the ability to go to a tighter choke, with the use of choke tubes or extra barrels, is even more important to the small-bore gunner. But as you reduce bore diameter, you must settle for reduced effectiveness at the longer ranges. A true full choke performer (70% patterns at 40 yards) is a rare item in a 20 gauge factory gun. You can achieve such effectiveness in some 3-inch 20 bores, but don't take the choke markings as gospel, especially if you want to use it for waterfowl.

If you don't want to be bothered patterning, settle in your mind that 40 yards is your really critical range and try not to stretch it. With the 28 gauge you'll have to lose another five yards, but since you won't be using this for ducks, I hope, you can still feel safe with it on upland birds at 35 yards. And lest I sound too restrictive, pace off the next half-dozen quail or woodcock or grouse you kill, both those with the first shot and those with the second. And remember that we're talking the limits of <u>effective</u> patterns, those that will come close to having one pellet for every two square inches in a 30-inch circle. Your 20 gauge, for example, that is bored improved cylinder should have one pellet in every two square inches at 25 yards with number 9 shot. At 35 yards, you'll need full choke with your ⅞ ounce load of 9's to get the same result. Anything less than this <u>is not</u> an effective pattern.

I've noticed lately that I seem to spend a lot more time looking for birds than have been hit with open chokes than those hit with a bit more shot. The shooter tends to blame his gun, the shells, or his breakfast. What is hard to come to grips with is that after age 40 or 45 we are inclined to be five yards slower, for one or more reasons – even for not being as competitive or intense.

I must admit I hesitated before so drastically altering a rather nice side-by-side with choke tubes, but this is more or less my everyday shooter, and an extra set of barrels is expensive, cumbersome to travel with, and it's rare that both pairs of barrels will feel the same.

Of course, many guns now manufactured offer the availability of extra choke tubes. In my opinion this "extra" is probably the greatest technical advance in the last 50 years. Not only are the tubes practical in terms of handiness and low cost, but they work as effectively, if not more so, than integral chokes. Virtually all manufacturers offer them as an option on at least some of their models.

My hearing problem has forced me to put away a favorite little 28 bore that's bored skeet in both barrels. Next fall, it'll have choke tubes in it – modified and full.

The race does not always go to the swift.

The
British
Best

I am delighted to see that a good many shooters lately are interested in fine English guns and want to know where they can be found, what are they, and how much. A good English gun is expensive by any standard, and prices continue to rise. But if you want to own and shoot the "best," then here's some of what you are faced with.

Commonly I'm asked about buying guns abroad in Britain and I, commonly, suggest that you don't. Guns are not less expensive in England, for one reason; another is the red tape from U.S. Customs, not to mention duty costs. More importantly, if you find that you have a truly bad gun, rare but possible, you have little recourse, and what you do have is riddled with aggravation.

The most familiar names of best guns are Purdey and Holland & Holland, with Boss (probably the best of the three) coming in a distant third. Just to set a base line, I believe that the current price of a Purdey side-by-side is over that of a couple cars with a wait of about three years. Holland is about the same, and the Boss company is so derelict that I hesitate to even consider them as a current maker.

The list of relatively unfamiliar names of superb guns is long and almost impossible to list accurately since so many made so few guns that their reputations, although flawless, were also fleeting. But among the ones you would be most likely to see and can feel assured of the highest quality are these: Atkin, Churchill, Beesley, Bland, Evans, Lang, Grant, Dickson, Greener, Westley Richards, Cogswell & Harrison, Hussey, Scott, Woodward, Lancaster, and Horsely. Some of these are Birmingham guns and some are London guns. The more prestigious have the London address – since that's where the money was and where the gentry came to be fitted.

Some of these guns are boxlocks and some are sidelocks – the boxlock being much less expensive but functionally on a par with the sidelock. The difference? Well, the sidelock is <u>nicer</u> – it looks better and lends itself to quality engraving, but it also offers perfect trigger pulls and the knowledge of intricate and superb handwork – part of the ephemeral quality that adds grace and balance and supports the term "best." (It is not uncommon to see the interior of a sidelock proudly engraved with the name of the lock maker.) This has long been the subject of controversy and I can't settle it one way or another; I own and shoot both but if money weren't a problem, I would unhesitatingly choose the sidelock.

A "best" gun is handmade – lock, stock, and barrel, commonly by specialists with years and years of apprenticeship and craft: stockers, barrel strikers, regulators, etc. Commonly, the assembled gun was finally passed by a shop foreman or by the man who had his name on the plates who was relentless in searching for flaws. If it weren't "best," it was fixed or it didn't leave the shop.

I might remind you that all the metal parts were hand filed

from a block of steel, and the final fitting was done to a wisp of smoke from an oil lamp – I have one such gun that is over a hundred years old, has seen considerable use, and if you placed a piece of tissue paper over the face of the receiver, the gun won't close. That is craftsmanship!

The reason, in the main, for the demise of so many fine names is that the men were craftsmen first and businessmen second. They simply couldn't afford to make guns of that quality and charge as little as they did, and it wasn't until the last 15 years or so that Purdey, always the bellweather of the trade, dramatically raised its prices. But by then many of the names I've listed were long gone.

What should you be cautious about? Primarily that the gun has been proofed in England for 2¾-inch shells, or has been bored out by a competent gunsmith to take this length of shell; most British 12-gauge shells were (and still are) only 2½-inches long. I wouldn't reject one because of short chambers; it's easily fixed except for the very rare thin-walled barrel; better yet, 2½-inch shells are becoming very available here. And since there is still a little larceny and/or ignorance around, I would insist, in buying from anyone, an inspection period of several days and have one or more good gunsmiths check the hinge pin, bores, and locks.

I would not reject a gun because of a little bore pitting or a scratched or worn stock or the normal cosmetic blemishes that happen over a period of time – they can be fixed or ignored. One more major, but very uncommon, fault is a double that shoots way off the point of aim; that's a cause for total rejection unless the gun is such a bargain that a new set of barrels won't be prohibitive in your total investment.

Briefly, I would consider a fine gun with Damascus barrels – many gunshops do re-sleeving. I would consider, very readily, an outside hammer gun – often at a substantial savings, as I would also not quibble about not having ejectors; although non-ejectors are common in hammer guns, they are rare in best-quality sidelocks. An original fitted case is nice, but not a must. The original chokes will probably be fairly open, variations on improved cylinder and modified are common, but if the choking is too full, it can be relieved without affecting the value of the gun.

I have been informed that if the chokes are relatively open, the use of steel shot is not destructively abrasive. One friend has shot many hundreds of steel shot loads through his Holland & Holland with no noticeable damage. An extra set of barrels to accommodate steel shot is, of course, an easily available item – but plan on spending some good money.

Most English guns are stocked a bit longer and a bit straighter than we are used to. Personally, I prefer such a stock and have a preference for the slight cast-off that is common as well. Ordinarily, the gun will have double triggers, a straight-hand stock, 28-inch barrels, and weigh less than seven pounds. Over-unders are rather scarce, usually premium priced, and except for certain makes (Boss, Woodward, Westley Richards), I would treat them with caution; some of the older Purdey over-unders are a never-ending source of trouble. The same holds for single-trigger guns; some are fine, some are not, and you should treat each gun on its own merits. In general, the British single trigger is a question mark. But again, several American shops can convert double triggers to fine single ones if you can't live without one.

To sum up this too-brief look at British shotguns, I only wish I'd had one years ago – no, make that several guns, and as long as we're just wishing, make one of them a sidelever Grant.

Hammer
Guns

The following is about something that you probably don't want, is hard to come by, impractical by modern standards, and was considered "obsolete" long before 1900. However, since you probably don't have anything all that much better to do for the next few minutes, what's the harm in indulging me in another of my bizarre excursions...a visit to the small and nearly forgotten world of the hammer gun.

The brief history of the modern shotgun as we know it actually began as recently as 1866. By this time we had two major improvements: the patent for modern-type centerfire cartridges (1861) and W.R. Pape's applied theory of choke boring (this is arguable, but let's not bother right now). So everything was ready for the final touches, which were the Purdey patents for underlocking lugs and the coming of breechloaders in 1870. By 1875, these ideas had altered the whole shotgun industry and almost all the guns made were top opening lever, drop-down barrels – with exposed hammers. The early barrels were, of course, Damascus steel. But by 1880, "best" guns began appearing with Sir Joseph Whitworth's

Fluid Pressed Steel barrels that were "nitro proofed"; essentially the side-by-side we know today – give or take the lovely serpentine curves of the artfully engraved hammers. Already (by 1875) the boxlock hammerless creations of Anson & Deeley were evident, and the "best" guns were being produced in that version. In 1885 we had the creation and acceptance of Needham's reliable ejector system. So, almost as quickly as it arrived, the hammer gun was obsolete: from 1875 to 1880 with Damascus barrels, and from 1880 to 1885 with the option of fluid steel.

However, in the brief 10 years when the "best" guns were made with hammers, they created a broad following of superb shots, including British royalty, who swore by them – no doubt as much for their graceful and functional appearance as for their reliability.

Many shooters still insisted on exposed hammers as late as the 1920s when all but the odd one or so ceased being made. The few that were made in the last years were for eccentric gunners or those hardy souls who demanded a shotgun that was strong, easily repaired, and yet of high quality for their journeys to the far corners of the world.

The guns made in America followed the same line of progression and change, as did the ones from continental Europe.

As the hammerless gun became the darling of the sporting gentlemen, the old hammer models were passed on to the gamekeeper or were discarded as dangerous – simply thrown out or put away to gracefully rust themselves into oblivion. Almost, but not quite.

A few shooters found themselves in the same position that I found myself in a few years ago – of wanting a best-quality gun and being totally unable to afford a hammerless gun of that quality. Some shooters, mostly Americans, saw the lines of beauty in these fine guns and continued to use them in spite of their unfashionability – or perhaps <u>because</u> of it. Notable among these were several live pigeon shooters of the first rank who stayed with their old Purdeys or an equivalent, and quite a few of the Southern gentry who still found their old hammer guns – often in 20 or 28 gauge – just as delightful to gun quail with or to pleasure themselves with in the dove field as ever. One very famous shooter that I know still maintains and frequently uses one or another of his collection of over a hundred.

Today's market for fine quality hammer guns with fluid steel barrels is small, especially based on the number of those available, even more so in the more desirable smaller gauges. There were many made in 20, 28, and .410, as well as 10, 12, and 16 gauge, and a sprinkling of 24's and 32's on the one side and 8's and 6's on the other. I've even seen a matched pair of 4 bores, complete with reloading tools and all the accessories. They were lovely...and whoever was man enough to handle them has my undying admiration.

With our modern methods of gunsmithing, even the old Damascus-barreled guns, if of good quality otherwise, are being coveted. For a reasonable amount of money these can be re-barreled or sleeved or even fitted with tubes to be a smaller gauge – 16 gauges made into 20's, and 20's fitted with 28-gauge tubes – much like the familiar skeet sets long offered by Jess Briley, Kohler, and others.

If the gun were of fine quality, I would have little hesitation in doing almost any restoration work to make it a shooter. The cost of a new stock or a new set of barrels is far, far below what the intrinsic value of such a gun might well be. If a stock is in good condition and the problem is one of fit, there are many places where such a stock can be bent to where it is perfectly suitable, including niceties of fit like cast-on, cast-off or toe-in and toe-out.

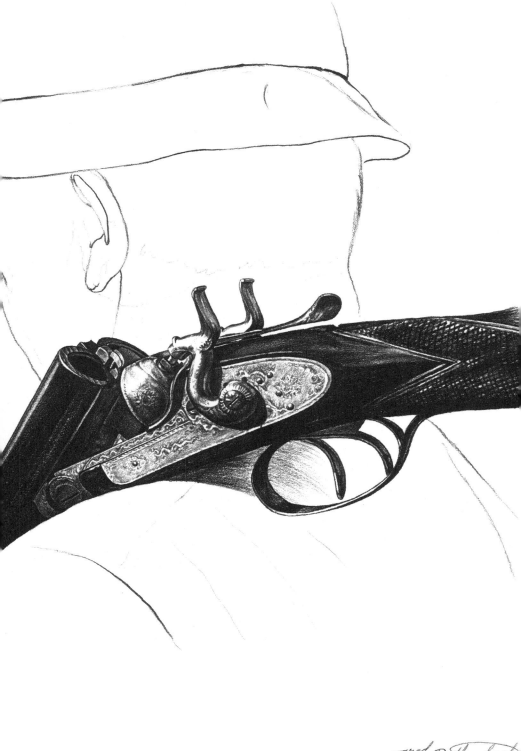

Fred Rothenbush

If it were of lesser quality – say an old Remington or low-grade Parker – I would be a bit more careful how much money I put into it. I would have it examined carefully by a gunsmith first and have an estimate or two done. I did own an old Remington that was a bit on the shabby-looking side, but after about $50 worth of work – including stock bending – I had a delightful duck gun that I very much enjoyed using.

Of course, the hammer gun has built-in liabilities. They very rarely came with ejectors; I've never seen one, although they do exist. Another question is that of safety. Hunting over a pointing dog presents little problem, since the gun need not be cocked until you're ready to shoot. To uncock it, I simply open it up and let the hammers down when the gun is "broken."

Admittedly, having a hammer gun for a now-and-then outing is somewhat of an indulgence, but there are worse and less satisfying ones. I liken it in a way to using a fine bamboo fly rod – both are functional pieces of art. Both can give us as much pleasure to own as a painting might, as well as that rare thrill of allowing us to slip a little back into history and be able to experience virtually first-hand what it was like to be afield in the times of Edward VII.

As collector's items, I feel that the fine hammer guns will be outstanding. There were so few made and they were made so well that those who can afford to have one will find it a far more liquid investment than many of the more modern counterparts. I personally know of several quality hammer guns that were selling a few years ago in the area of $1,000 that are now priced at well over $10,000. I saw a Purdey hammer gun at an English auction house last fall, one that needed a bit of work here and there, and found out that it sold to a dealer for almost $17,000! Outrageous? Maybe, and maybe not.

Luckily, there are still a few dealers who have good hammer gun sense and have a few on hand most of the time. Like any fine piece, these old guns aren't inexpensive and haven't been for a while, but it's still possible to get a superb working gun for a fraction of what you'd expect to pay for a similar name and quality in a hammerless model.

Not the least of the charms of having a hammer gun is that to the untrained eye (i.e., most wives) it is obviously an antique and not the sort of equipment that shrieks mindless extravagance. On the contrary – a man can bring one home, proudly display it, and begin a discourse on his personal new trend toward economy and thrift. One should, however, take a bit more care to cover his tracks than one person whom I know all too well. He saved his gunsmith bills, including having one new hammer made, and forgot to note that the man doing the work had mentioned that this particular gun was worth several thousands and that he'd be willing to buy it if it were ever up for sale – and his wife wired it into a floor lamp, showing me for the thousandth time that there is no such thing in this world as an unmixed blessing. Or, as our old friend Mr. Shakespeare put it, "O what a tangled web we weave when first we practice to deceive…"

Guns
as
Investments

In 1927 Paul Curtis, who was shooting editor of "Field & Stream," wrote an article for the Stoeger gun catalog about fine shotguns as an investment. At the time, you could buy a good American made double gun for less than a hundred dollars and the best of the London guns for around a thousand. Using the blessing of hindsight, we now know that what Captain Curtis wrote was true. I needn't go into what our economy was like in those years just preceding the Great Depression. Although I believe that the incremental differences in cost are not too dissimilar to our present times, I don't believe that the investment parallels are any longer applicable.

Today the <u>best</u> guns made, or at least the most expensive, are for argument's sake the British Purdey and the Italian Fabbri; both are selling for just about <u>$35,000</u>. Of course, world trade and the international money market are factors but I doubt that, as an investment, a $35,000 gun would rank very high with the man who manages your or my account.

To come down to a level that is more understandable, we

have the older "best" guns like the Purdey, Boss, Woodward, and Holland from abroad and the Winchester 21 and Parkers at the top of the domestic market with a variety of models and grades of the Smiths, Ithacas, and the like scattered over the market with prices that vary like the commodities exchange. But although the new gun prices have escalated, the "old" prices have not kept anywhere near parallel.

The 12 bore Model 21 in fine condition in an ordinary model – nothing fancy in the way of engraving or wood – has stayed pretty much at a constant level. While a fine and ultra-serviceable gun, I sincerely doubt that a person can reasonably expect the gun to accrue very much in monetary terms beyond what it has.

If you like a Model 21 and can afford one, it would be a good buy but not, in my opinion, an investment with great possibility of profit. I feel this way about all the old American doubles, that they have come close to peaking out in the market. I haven't seen a real bargain in a couple of years.

In the British makers the used gun bargains are just as rare. The famous names are in the $10,000 class and only those who look hard will find one of the many fine but lesser-known makers like Lang, Hussey, Grant, or Horsely, to name but a few that are about half the cost of the Purdeys and Bosses but in general their equal in quality and function.

The point is that the time for buying investment guns is probably past. But as Captain Curtis pointed out 30 years ago, "The sportsman should not consider his arms from a cold and mercenary point of view. He does not buy them for profit, but for service, and he should therefore write off a certain amount for service rendered. Nevertheless, a fine weapon will, if wisely disposed of, fetch closer to its purchase price than a cheap gun would; and a really fine one will, if held long enough, frequently bring more."

If the good investment era is about over, what Curtis wrote still makes a lot of common sense. Today we have a wide choice of excellent double guns from Spain, Italy, and the Continent as well as some made in Japan that are of heirloom quality even if not "guaranteed" to increase in value.

Even these good guns are gradually creeping up in cost, and if I were contemplating a new gun in this category, I wouldn't wait any longer than necessary. The gun isn't going to get any more valuable just because its price is going up. Last year I was contemplating ordering a good Italian gun, and by the time I made up my mind to go ahead based on the "you only live once" theory, the price had risen by another $1,000 due to currency fluctuations and an escalation in labor costs. I canceled my order and decided that I could live with what I've got. Maybe if I get lucky I'll find one in the used gun lists that's close to what I could have ordered new if I'd been a little smarter...or richer...or quicker.

One of the problems in the gun market is that the so-called traditionalists, myself included, have made so much of the niceties of the double gun that there seems to be some magic attached to any gun of that design. Of course that just isn't so. More junker double guns have been produced by far than any other kind, and some makers carry the magic over into the cost – or try to. I can't tell you how often someone has trotted out his father's or grandfather's old double and stood by waiting for ravishing words of praise for a gun that wouldn't be out of place in a hen house for rat control. A lot of these old clunkers were marked with such subterfuge as "Holland" or "Purdy" or whatever, and a numberless amount are simply marked Fabrique en Belgique, which should translate to, "Let the buyer beware."

While there are a few guns that might make you money and many that won't lose their value, there are a lot that aren't worth even thinking seriously about – including some new ones. I've seen some late model stuff from Europe so poorly designed it was painful to even think about shooting any of them. You can live with a pump or auto that really doesn't fit the way you'd like, but a double that's too light (and some of the later 20 bores are), or too small in the trigger guard, or too sharp in the comb is a very, very punishing shotgun. And these are just a few of the more common faults – from makers who think that just because the barrels are side-by-side they've made a field gun. At almost any price, these are no bargains.

I yearned to be a traditionalist, longing for a sleek side-by-side, long before I could afford one. But the years of lugging my Model 12 pump and an even less responsive over-under later on only whetted my appetite for something special. When the time finally arrived, I told myself that I was not only acquiring a good gun, I was making a prudent investment. I did keep the gun longer than I would have held onto that much cash, and I did manage to sell it for a bit more than I paid. But I sold it because I couldn't hit very well with it. The only real investment profit I made with that clumsy double is that it forced me to do my homework and learn what it was I didn't like about some guns and did like about others. I still don't have this down as tight as I'd like, but then I don't know too many others who do; I believe that we're all to one degree or another experimenters, fickle about this or that and often reluctant to admit a wrong choice.

I believe that only after you have a good idea of what you will really enjoy in the way of a good shotgun should you make a large capital investment. Then, if you know you'll be happy with it and can afford it, go ahead. Don't delude yourself that all guns are money in the bank; even if they are, they're not a liquid as you might wish – as any good gun dealer will testify.

I will let the (almost) last word belong to Captain Curtis: "I have considerable pity...for the man who cannot, or will not, see the value of a fine shotgun, for he is losing a lot of the pleasure which shooting affords its devotees – the satisfaction of doing the thing right..."

I see the gun buyer getting a lot more sophisticated, however, and rightly so. The influx of fine guns reasonably priced is a function of the new interest in quality – not just a name. Hopefully, this trend will continue to grow and free market competition will send prices back at least a little to where we can pick and choose more freely, and value and cost will come closer together than in the recent past.

If you're in the market, shop around; take advantage of the trial period that reputable dealers offer. Make a counter proposal. Don't do it for dreams of profit, but for pleasure, satisfaction, and perhaps because you only live once.

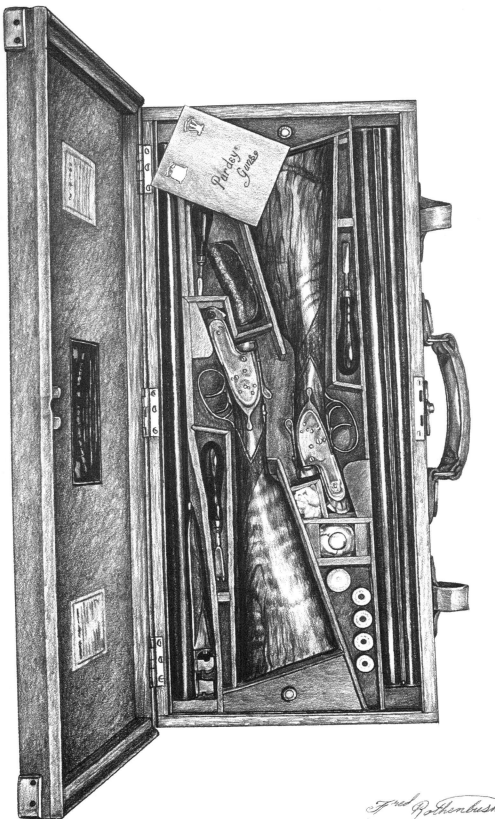

Purdey
Guns

Fred Rothenbush '89

They were Built to Be Used

Ono of the really hard decisions some of the luckier of us have to face is what to do with that old Parker or L. C. Smith or Ithaca – or even a Purdey or some other fine English or European gun. Do you keep it, sell it, shoot it, or just take it out and look at it every so often?

You might as well ask my opinion about drawing two cards to a flush – I'll give an answer based on what I know and how I feel, but it's your money! A couple of old and good guns that I own, I shoot. Another scratch in the stock or a shade less bluing isn't going to lessen the long-run value in the event I want to sell or trade. But these guns fit me, I bought them to use, and I get a great deal of pleasure out of using them. If I owned an old Rolls, I'd drive it.

What about one of your old-timers that you'd like to shoot, but it doesn't fit? Well, you're faced with a decision that costs in the neighborhood of $500 and up. That's if you want to save the original stock and have a new one made. The old stock must be kept for the integrity of the gun, but if the chance to use and enjoy a good-grade double appeals to you, then the money will be well spent. I don't know of any high-grade guns that sell for that kind of money, and my personal choice would probably be to have new wood (utility grade) made and enjoy the heirloom. I might not trust it to the airlines or take it out in the salt marshes, but use it I would, with the exception of one of the exotic or extraordinarily fancy grades.

Common sense ought to raise its rare head – but I think that far too many usable and enjoyable firearms are made into museum pieces when there's no reason not to hunt with them.

Now, what about the shotgun that's Grandpa's old live pigeon or duck gun – the one with 32-inch barrels that throw patterns around 90 percent? I'll tell you what I did with mine: I sent it to England to have a new set of barrels made so I can use it for upland birds. The new barrels are identical to the old – the same wide-filed rib and weight – except they will be 28 inches and bored improved cylinder and a light modified. This is a fairly expensive procedure and takes about six months, but I dearly love the old gun and, after weighing all the options, decided that I'd rather invest a bit more and have a gun that I could use a lot rather than have a good gun that I couldn't really use at all.

If you've got a fine, old gun that happens to have Damascus barrels, I'd seriously consider doing the same thing or having them sleeved so that it would be safe to use modern ammunition. Such new barrels or sleeved ones are, of course, tested with the heavy proof loads and so marked. Any old gun that's been sitting around for an appreciable time ought to be thoroughly checked out by a good gunsmith before you use it. I would want to know something about the work and reputation of a person before I'd let him do any interior surgery or exploration on one of my good guns. I've seen some absolutely disgraceful jobs – ones that nearly ruined the value of the gun, especially when it comes to rebluing. Bluing is something that is not absolutely necessary – <u>don't, don't, don't</u> do it unless you are absolutely positive that the barrels won't be scored with wire brushes, etc.

A first-class craftsman will usually insist that whatever engraving was on the barrels, such as the maker's name, address, etc., be re-engraved so that layers of bluing don't build up and obscure the fine details that help give the gun its value. But do check for weak or broken springs, extractors, firing pins, etc. All these can be replaced – and are probably better than new with today's metallurgy – without compromising the real value of the piece.

Don't forget to check the trigger pulls. Your grandfather may have been a logger and felt that about nine pounds was just right; you are probably used to three or four. It wouldn't hurt to save all the old pieces if some do need to be replaced, just in case some collector someday may want them for whatever bizarre reason.

What about changing the existing chokes if everything else seems to suit you? I've asked some of our more prestigious gun dealers, and they feel that it really doesn't make all that much difference – providing you don't alter the original length of the barrels.

I think that a full-and-full or full-and-modified could be opened in one barrel, the first one fired, of course, to improved cylinder or a light modified without fear. A lot of the old guns were fearfully tight and with today's superb shotshells, they're even tighter. Do a little test firing with your favorite loads first, then find a reputable gunsmith – not a hobbyist – and have it done right.

I assume you will check the chamber length first and make sure that it's cut for 2¾-inch shells because, as you know, many British and European guns were made for 2½-inch shells in

12 gauge and 2⁹/₁₆ inch in 16 gauge. Many of the older guns were also proofed for one ounce loads, and this must be checked as well. The opinion of a good gunsmith here, as well, is invaluable.

Being a 16 gauge fan, I have a couple of short-chambered guns: one an old Browning auto and the other a side-by-side. Both were lengthened to 2¾ inches, and both work fine with light field loads.

Where "reconditioning" is concerned, here are the things you must consider: What is the gun worth as it is now – is it sensible to spend more money on it? Will I shoot it enough to make an additional investment worthwhile? Am I going to ruin the integrity of the gun, or am I actually going to increase its value?

Naturally, I can't help you here. I'm neither a gun appraiser nor a gunsmith. But if you have a gun that you believe is of above average value, find someone who is reputable and ask his opinion (and offer to pay for it). There are a couple of other considerations; one is that a gun believed to be of value may really not be worth all that much – there are an awful lot of junkers and imitations floating around; two, the gun may be of great value and you'd best either keep it as it is or sell it and get something you can use. And don't be shy about getting more than one opinion if you aren't satisfied; it's your money at the bottom line.

Bear in mind through all of this what good guns sell for these days – it's mind-staggering, and if you have one that will give you pleasure with the addition of a couple of hundred dollars or more worth of improvements, it just might be the best thing you can do with it. Shooting and honest outside wear is harmless compared to the sense of rightness in having a fine, old smoothbore out there, shooting the way it was intended to when it was made. Think how pleased some oldtimer would be if he knew that his pet is once more someone's pride and joy.

The
28 Gauge –
A Thing
of Beauty

No one has ever asked me what I thought would make the ideal woodcock and grouse gun (you probably wanted my opinion but it slipped your mind). It's a good thing too, because what I would prefer now is a little different from what I thought was just the ticket a few years ago.

In my part of the East during my formative years, the real sports either owned, or were planning to, a 16 gauge bird gun. Those with the money went with the Parker for the most part, but there were plenty of L.C. Smiths and Ithacas that got trotted out for inspection in the general store. Those of us with no earthly prayer of ever being able to spend over a hundred dollars for a shotgun went with the Browning auto "Sweet Sixteen" or rummaged around for a Winchester Model 12 or even a Model 97. But it was a 16 gauge or stay sleepless.

As time went on, too much of it as it happened, I finally got my 16 whose praises I will still sing, but like a lot of things I always wanted, it came in a bit late, for by then the thing to have if you were a gentleman gunner was a 20 bore.

Needless to say, prices had escalated across the board. The once hundred-dollar guns were now two or three times that if you wanted a double, and we all really did. But again a lot of us had to draw the line somewhere and we went with current fashion with the Model 12 again, or the Remington pump. (No doubt all of us who did later sold them, and no doubt again, all of us regret it.) These little 20-gauge pumps were pretty slick; good pointing, a bit too heavy, but as reliable as anyone could ever ask. You couldn't go wrong then with one and the same still holds true; plus a few decent autoloaders in lightweight models are readily available.

Now anyone who ended up with one of these 16's or 20's and still has it ought to be delighted; no question that they'll get the job done, and all the reasons you bought one are just as valid.

But if bird hunters were normal people I wouldn't be writing this and neither would you be reading it. It's not that I really think I'll shoot any better – nothing practical like that – but I have been serpent-bit, as they used to say, and I am practically back to exactly the same emotional place that I was when I would lie awake figuring out how much extra wood I'd have to cut or what fur I could trap to get what I didn't think I could live without.

Now I'm absolutely convinced (no more changing my mind!) that for small-bird gunning I'll do as well with a 28 gauge as I can do with a 20. All this started several years ago in a dove field in Mexico, an ideal situation to get pragmatic about the capabilities of a gun because of virtually unlimited birds, meaning that you could choose to shoot certain angles or only incomers and be assured of plenty of just what you wanted and know precisely enough at what yardage you were taking your shots.

I've long felt that the 28 was one of those strange creatures, like the incredible .375 H&H Magnum rifle, that performs a great deal better in the field than can be proved on paper. Ballisticians can, and do, prove anything they want, so I preferred to do the shooting myself and search out the opinions of gunners that I considered both objective and superior shots.

I have by now taken hundreds of doves with the 28 at ranges of 25 to 40 yards and have satisfied myself that if you can point it where it should be, you'll get positive and clean kills. I talked to many of our finest skeet shooters and they all agree that – given as much experience with the 28 as with the 20 – they'd shoot it just as well, and several thought they'd do better.

My starting to shoot heavily with the 28 wasn't done on a whim or idle curiosity. When you do a lot of firing, as you will on flighting doves with high legal limits, the average 20 bore has quite a lot of bite. And more than one I've shot is positively mean; especially with the one-ounce load. So I was looking for comfort combined with efficiency. For our upland gunning on grouse, quail, and woodcock, if you'll grant that our average shot rarely passes 35 yards, you sacrifice nothing in the way of performance and can shade the gun weight down half a pound or better, thus gaining some extra seconds for more careful shooting and having just that much less to lug around in heavy cover.

One of the magic qualities of the 28 is the fact that the bore diameter and the ¾-ounce load seem to be a perfect ballistic match. The patterns are not only superbly efficient at 35 yards in modified barrels, but the shot string is much shorter than that of the one-ounce load in a similarly choked 20 gauge. If you talk to an experienced 28 gauge fan and he tells you that he just feels that his little gun "hits harder," he's right; and the brief shot string is a good deal of the answer why.

We all know that it's pattern – not choke – that is the proof of the pudding and that a .410 will put all of its shot load in a 30" circle as well as a 12 gauge will. There is just less of it. In the case of the 28 gauge, let me assure you that there's plenty of pattern efficiency for the shooter who wants a light and pleasant gun.

As I've mentioned before, anyone who wants to go to a lighter gun has to realize that he must learn to make certain adjustments. Since the laws of Newton are still unrepealed, you have to bear in mind that the easier it is to start a gun barrel in motion, the easier it is to check or stop it. One of the common complaints of a gunner going away from his old 12 gauge is that the new "little gun," be it a 20 or 28, has to be handled according to its weight, and it can be absolutely unforgiving to the unsmooth pointer. You must remember to swing through. The gun isn't going to do it for you as it will in a heavier gauge. You ought to have that habit anyway regardless of what you're using, but that's one of the reasons the heavier guns let us get away with making a mistake.

As you become accustomed to the lighter and faster guns, you'll find that you can be quite precise, and since you will be on your bird a fraction faster, you have that much more time to swing through and make your shot just when you want to. My old 16 that I mentioned earlier only weighs about 5½ pounds and was made with 24" barrels and that combination means that you have to do all the work, and the least bit of nonchalance can be very embarrassing indeed.

One of the adjustments in your shooting style that I suggest you try if you experience any difficulties with a lighter gun is to change the position of your hand holding the barrels. A short hold will give you a faster move, and extending your grip will help slow you down. No doubt you've seen photographs of the typical English shooter with his left hand way out past the forearm – just remember that he's very likely a very accomplished game shot and that he's most likely shooting a gun that weighs in the area of only six to 6½ pounds.

Am I saying that a 28 is the ideal gun? Not at all. I use the 12 as a basic, as do most of us, not because it is ideal but because it's both efficient and practical. All I offer here is another look at a shotgun dimension that seems, sadly, to be leaving us.

The economics of the gun business are harsh, and no marketing man in his right mind would suggest to a maker that a sleek 28 would have the American gunner beating a path to his door. But the 28 is a thing of beauty – practical, efficient, and quickly becoming a "ghost" gun...the kind we see flickering in the log fires of our favorite places when the talk turns to those sweet subjects when we ask "What if..."

"What if..." I could order one for myself right this minute? Let it be a side-by-side, of course. Straight-hand English stock, splinter forearm, 28" barrels, double triggers, and both barrels bored modified or perhaps modified and improved modified. A handsome bit of scroll engraving on the side plates and – on the bottom of the receiver – a soaring woodcock done in gold. And, if you'll forgive a slight eccentricity (not the rarest thing in the hunting field), I think I'll ask for outside hammers just because I love the way they look; not a must, mind you, but just a part of the dream.

Would I shoot better? Unlikely, but that's not the point. It's just one of those things that makes us bird hunters; another part of the dream of soft mornings, classic dogs, and just enough flushes to make us say when it's all over, "This is what I want to remember, this is what it's all about."

The Sixteen –
Still Sweet

If I were to sit down and make a list of what might be the ideal requirements for an upland gunner's shotgun, my ideas would include a few facts and a few fancies. An ounce of shot ought to be enough, and 2½ drams of powder plenty to propel it. That dictates a gun that weighs no more than six or 6½ pounds; light enough to carry, quick enough to swing, yet with enough weight to have an essential momentum for smoothness and to take the bite from the recoil.

Another essential of my upland gun is that it appeal to the eye as well as to the hand. A straight or half-pistol grip, a delicate slimness to the receiver and barrels, and one or two triggers depending on your preference. No harm in a bit of engraving to relieve the eye and add a touch of distinction, and we could carry this a bit further and checker the end of the buttstock or fit a skeleton bit of metal for protection against wear and handling. And what would we have? That almost-forgotten darling of a few generations past: the 16 gauge.

You don't have to agree that this would be an ideal gun. Obviously not many do, for the 16-gauge shells in your gunsmith's shop or the hardware store are likely covered in dust and take up only a row or two in a neglected corner.

Just what happened to the 16? Well, the very ideals that created it were carried almost to excess, and instead of gunners having the dilemma of catering to two loves, they settled on one – and that, as you know, was the 20 bore.

In the minds of the decision makers – the gun and ammunition companies – everything that separated the 16 from the 12 came to separate the 16 from the 20. Sleekness and lightness? That's the 20? An ounce of shot or a bit more or less? That's the 20. And while I might have made a good case that too often the 20 was too light and was used to fire larger charges than are comfortable, almost no one would listen.

The ammunition companies, long eager to find a reason to reduce the almost incredible number of gauges and loadings that they had to carry, saw the 20 as the salvation. The research and development lads brushed the 16 aside and sold an audience, eager for something new, on the idea that anything the 16 – and a lot of 12's – could do, the 20 could handle as well. And the "modern" American upland gunner bought it. If quickness was desirable, let's have the quickest possible; if lightness was good, let's have the lightest. The old 16's of their fathers were trotted down to the gun stores by the thousands and traded in on the new paragon. Friends came over and admired the new acquisitions and became, in turn, members of the True Faith.

In its time, the 16 was the darling of the upland gunner, the kind of man you saw on the old calendars rather nattily attired and as often as not wearing a necktie. He was invariably flanked by a brace of bird dogs with setters favored in the Yankee hillsides and pointers drifting along quail covers spotted by spires of pine trees with tumbling corncribs and plank cabins in the background. The fanciers of the 16 argued, with a lot of sense, that the 12 gauge was a waterfowl gun, the 20 ideal for ladies and youngsters, and the 16 the unavoidable choice for the <u>experienced</u> bird shooter.

Most of the American gun companies that catered to the 16 fancier did it the easy way, by screwing 16-gauge barrels on 12-gauge receivers and thus doing next to nothing for the man who wanted a lighter gun than a 12 but something just a little more substantial than a 20. The "real" 16, long a standard in Europe, was often a Francotte from Belgium, a product of Ulm in Germany, or imported from France or Britain. At home, we had the Parker, primarily, and of course the traditional L.C. Smith, Fox, Baker, et al., along with the neatly sculptured Model 21 Winchester.

The only true 16's done as autoloaders were made by Browning in Belgium. Their "Sweet Sixteen" was a favorite pet of duck hunters as well as partridge and quail men – and no doubt still is to those few smart enough to hang onto them.

The only real effort made by the big American companies was to improve the 12 and extend the range of loads for the 20 and sort of hope that the 16 would go away; the policy of benign neglect gradually had its intended result.

No doubt the majority of gun writers would say, and who can blame them, that the loss of the 16 is a trifle. They can point out that the modern 20 has 3-inch chambers and you can still get loads that run from less than an ounce up to 1¼ in them, and so what good is the old 16? There's no really valid argument in the 20 vs. 16 from a pure ballistical standpoint. You can wave <u>almosts</u> around all you want, but it makes no difference to the quail or grouse or woodcock whether he's centered by an ounce of 8's from a 16 or from a 20.

The 16 being a bit larger in bore diameter (.670) than the 20 (.615) and likely a shade heavier would certainly have less felt recoil, but not that much less, especially to the gunner swinging on a fast-moving blur of brown feathers. There really isn't much logic to the 16, but I find that there's still a lot of love.

Where the 16 excels, and again this is purely in the eyes of the beholder, is in its almost perfect lines. Where the run-of-the-mill 12 tends to be bulkier and heavier than it has to be, and the ordinary 20 is as often too light as it is too coarse, the true 16 is a fine example of the creed, "form follows function."

In my opinion, there is no need, ever (pheasants aside), for an upland bird gun to require more than an ounce of shot or 2½ drams of powder. Bore this gun improved cylinder and modified or improved and full, and all there is left for you to do is point it properly.

When we insist on lightness and speed, we have to be fully conscious of the fact that we are likely to overswing the bird, then check a bit, and then either do it over or risk missing behind. The light, fast shotgun is a very hard taskmaster, but the momentum of the heavier gun tends to help us erase a little mistake here and there.

Going back through some of the older books on upland gunning, you'll find the 16 mentioned with great frequency. The famous "Little Gun" in William Harnden Foster's "New England Grouse Shooting" was a 16; that marvelous storyteller, Burton Spiller, shot a 16 Parker for so many years that at the end of his gunning, the traces of bluing along the barrels and the checkering in the grip and forend were indistinct and getting along toward invisible. Since I don't believe I can be corrected, I'll guess that more grouse and woodcock in the Northeast were taken with 16 gauges (probably Parkers) than with any other gun, and that the 16 most surely held its own when it came to numbers in the field on many of the most storied Southern quail plantations.

No doubt the initial popularity of the 16 came as a statement on sportsmanship among the "fancy" as much as a feeling that the 12 was a bit too much gun. And so indeed was the

20 gauge the next step as both a statement and a further move toward "fairness": the sporting chance.

It would be foolish and maudlin to insist that the 16 is irreplaceable; it obviously isn't. It had its day and now it seems that day is over. Yet, somehow, I feel a warm spot in my heart when I meet a man whiling away an afternoon over a couple of bird dogs and when we stop to chat, the sleek lines of his double gun whisper "Sixteen." There's a magic in it to him that has its roots in days probably, and sadly, no longer with us. It makes me wish that things were a bit different than they are – and glad to know that here and there is someone carrying a "little gun" as much out of affection, or more so, than a proven belief in its ballistics.

The
Upland
Shotgun

Standing in my gun rack, at least during hunting season, is a short-barreled, very light side-by-side of a respectable, if not "best," English make. It is surrounded by a variety of American pumps and automatics and, to the casual eye, the little shotgun stands out like a rose among thorns. Invariably, visitors ask if they can pick it up and look at it and when I tell them to go ahead, they swing it up to the shoulder and through an imaginary covey of quail or a rocketing partridge. When they do, I know that the dream of the light and fast shotgun has been rekindled in another heart.

What they never ask – absolutely never – is how it performs in the field – the bottom line. Actually, I don't do too badly with it in the field if I use it a lot and get used to the low moment of inertia – ease of getting it going, in other words – and if I constantly remind myself that a gun this easy to start is just as easy to stop. But it's the last gun I own that I'd attempt a decent round of skeet with, and it will never be in a duck blind or a dove field when the going is hot and heavy.

It's a special gun, built for snap shooting in the heavy alder and birch covers and for ease of toting up and down New England hillsides.

So to be fair and honest, the search for the ideal upland game gun means a gun of specialist function. I think we can agree that among its special functions is that it's easy to carry – meaning it has decent balance and doesn't weigh more than seven pounds and preferably a bit less – and handles a combination of powder and shot capable of killing a game bird at a distance of 35 yards or a bit beyond. Obviously, for all practical purposes (mostly financial), we're talking about a 20 bore. The normal English game gun is a 6½ pound 12 gauge with 27 or 28-inch barrels that uses a 2½-inch shell with one ounce or a bit more of shot. Lovely indeed, but you can't run down to your neighborhood hardware store or gun shop and buy one, and if you could, you couldn't easily buy the ammunition. What the British use so well is a 12 bore that very nearly conforms to the weight and effectiveness of our common 20 gauge; not exactly, mind you, but close enough so that we can get on with what's practical for us, right here and right now.

Before we get too practical, we will admit that almost all of us would prefer to do our gunning over Maggie or Buck or Lady with a sleek side-by-side or over-under. Whether or not they are all that more ideal in balance than a pump or auto is a personal matter, but they should certainly be fast enough to mount and smooth to swing. And in theory, they can be made lighter, having no magazine tube or breech bolt. All on the plus side of the ledger, agreed? We can even agree that, even though this sort of gun is rather expensive, we feel quality and enjoyment can justify the expense, at least to each other if not to our wives and/or bankers.

And, I hear you ask, just how effective is this light and fast 20 gauge? Let me say that it can do its job probably a lot better

than you can do yours! The one-ounce load of 7½ carries about 345 shot, and at 40 yards each pellet has a striking energy of close to two foot pounds; more than adequate for birds of the weight of grouse, quail, and woodcock, and sufficient for pheasant, although I personally would move up to number 6 shot for a bird of this weight and plumage. If you stuck with an ounce of 8's in the improved cylinder bore and an ounce of 7½'s in the modified barrel and limited your shooting to ranges under 40 yards, you have to give nothing away, in practicality, to the 12-gauge gunner – providing your patterns are of sufficient density at the maximum range to ensure four or more pellets in a bird.

However, as we all know, there's no such thing as a free lunch. Will this light and well-balanced gun make you a faster shot? It certainly can. Will it make you a better or more consistent shot? Maybe. As I mentioned before in talking about balance, because you lose the natural momentum that exists in a heavy (eight pounds or so) 12 gauge, you have to learn a new set of shooting habits. One trick is to try a longer hold with the left hand, if you're a right-handed shooter. One of the many theories for this is to get more of the gun weight between the hands, creating more "feel" and better control. And, of course, the one thing we all forget until it's too late is that we almost always have much more time than we think we do at the moment. How often can you look back and <u>know</u> that you fired the first shot by fright and the second one by sight? Take the extra second or two and make sure you have the gun mounted correctly and that you're looking at the bird <u>intently</u>, not shooting more or less randomly at a blur in the air.

I don't see anything wrong with a lightweight pump or auto. You can easily get one balanced to your personal taste. Stock adjustment isn't too difficult or expensive, and in the end either works very well. More than one gunner I know is going into the bird fields with one of these moderately priced guns because his old doubles have gotten so valuable, he's getting leery of tramping around the woods with one of them. That's a pity, but that's about where we are – or haven't you priced gun insurance lately?

But, even though we keep telling ourselves dreams don't cost too much, the vision of the dainty double seems to fade quite quickly at the familiar and honest sound of a couple of 7½'s being tucked away in our nicked and worn pumps and autos. Next time old Duke or Max The Wonderdog hits a point, don't worry about what you're using...just do what we usually do and remember that the powder will smell as pungent, and the retrieve will be just as proud.

The
Field
Gun

Now, all the talk of specialist function aside, one of the reasons that this book is here and that you and I are involved in it is that there isn't a whole lot of agreement on what constitutes the best all-around upland shotgun. Like any reasonable man, I have changed my mind here and there over the years – because of new technology and my getting smarter about what <u>ideal</u> is. Without too much quibbling about gauge, except for the .410, which in my opinion is not a field gun, here is where I'm at – at this minute. Sort of a summing-up process.

Choke: Improved cylinder, what our British friends call quarter-choke, since it ought to throw 50 percent patterns, give or take a hair, at 40 yards.

Barrel length: 28 inches in an over-under or side-by-side, providing that the gun balances well, at or close to the hinge pin, and that the weight is proportional – which we will come to next. In a pump or autoloader, 26 inches of barrel is enough since the long receiver serves several of the functions of barrel length.

Weight: I still hold with the old standard of 96 times the normally chosen shot charge. So in a 12 gauge using one ounce plus a fraction, I'd like a gun that weighed less than seven pounds. For the smaller gauges, the same equation can stand except that to drop below six pounds makes a gun slide close to the toy class and keeps it from being a truly effective tool as a hunting arm; very light guns are just too hard to control.

Stock: Except in competition guns, I prefer a slim, straight-hand grip for the butt. I've done this to a couple of repeaters – and a notable favorite now is my 870 Remington 28 gauge dove and quail gun. This makes the gun feel faster to me and makes my carry position easier and more comfortable. The comb ought to be a touch on the high side as I believe we would all shoot a bit better with a gun that throws its patterns slightly high, plus this allows (or forces) us to keep the bird in view above the barrels. Beware the stock that is too thick – one of the most common faults of the average gun – mass produced or not. A too-wide stock is like "pernicious anemia"; you don't really feel bad with it, and yet you don't feel good and it's almost impossible to put your finger on what's wrong. It's an overlooked detail and most of us learn to live with it, but if I had my options I'd take a stock on the thin side every time. Stock length is, of course, individual, but a decent guide is that your nose is a little more than two fingers' width from your thumb when the gun is properly mounted. I like a zero pitch butt and will go against the classicists by voting for a recoil pad, for adherence – not appearance.

Triggers: The great British makers liked to set the pulls at half the weight of the gun and I agree since that normally gives us between 3½ and four pounds; anything a lot lighter can be scary and anything much heavier will often make us pull the gun off the target in an effort to fire. Another nicety is where the trigger is positioned in the guard; the farther back, the better. With double triggers (a pet option of mine), you must have room for your fingers to move freely from one trigger to the other. I once had a gun with a slightly undersized trigger guard and smaller than normal triggers, and it drove me crazy. I sold the gun and later found out that it was made for a man with smallish hands – good gunsmiths took things like that into consideration as a matter of course many years ago and really good ones still do. I find that the standard pump and semiautomatics have decent trigger placements and good, roomy guards. The factory pulls are often atrocious; in this age of litigation, guns come out of the store with pull poundage more suited to King Kong than the average upland gunner. If you don't care for the curvature or placement of a trigger, many of them can be bent or repositioned by a gunsmith – not an enormous problem.

Extra touches: I like a gun with a raised rib. I admit to liking the looks of it as much as utilizing the function of eye-catching and/or heat dispersion. I like slim forends on doubles and slimmer-than-they-usually-are on repeaters. I like small ivory front beads and am indifferent to middle-of-the-rib beads. A shotgun ought not look like a space ship! I appreciate nice wood but would think twice about paying a lot extra for it, and the same goes for engraving. At one time I was big on buying extra barrels for my repeaters – now I'm big on choke tubes; they're cheaper, handier, and work as well or better.

There's an ephemeral quality to a fine gun that's almost impossible to explain. It's a combination of feel and balance where the weight is between the gunner's hands. You might call it <u>elegance</u>; some have it and others don't. I own an inexpensive and not overly handsome 28 side-by-side that has it, and I also have a fairly expensive and "famous" 12 gauge that doesn't. It's the touch that kept certain gunmakers busy and wasn't part of the destiny of others. It's often a personal evaluation, but, for example, I don't find that <u>something extra</u> in the old Parker 12 bores. They strike me as a touch clubby. Most 20 gauge Model 21's are a bit heavy, while most 16-gauge 21's are almost perfect, using the classic standards. As inexpensive and mass-produced as it is, the Remington 1100, especially in the skeet sizes, points beautifully, as did the old Model 12 Winchester; I consider them both too heavy for field guns in 12 gauge and marginal in the 20 but if you aren't too picky (and I don't mean to be), you sure have a lot of very satisfied company. I just wish they'd been made a little lighter and sleeker, but you can say that about almost every shotgun made here that was created for upland shooting. I can live with an eight-pound plus duck gun, but not one that hefty that I have to carry.

One question that keeps recurring when the discussion gets to good guns is, "Why are American guns so heavy?" The answer is that it's easier and cheaper to do "coarse" work than "fine." Are heavier guns that much more sturdy? Not necessarily – all they really are is heavier.

I was at a fairly big sporting clays shoot in Texas a couple of months ago, and after the competition was over a good shooter was complaining about how disappointed he was that he hadn't done better. I said I thought his gun was too heavy and not quick enough for some of the more demanding targets. He disagreed, so I went over to a friend who had a delightful 6½-pound, 28-inch barrel side by side – not a "best" gun, but certainly a very good one. I handed this to the man I'd been discussing "ideal" guns with and asked him to try it. He smoked the next six pair I threw for him and then he turned and said, "It's like the first time you taste a really great wine!" I can't think of a better way of putting it.

And while we all can't afford the ideal shotgun, it's still nice to know that they exist, and that with a little effort and work, we can have a gun that may not look like something from London but – when we close our eyes and swing it – it not only feels good, but we know it will work.

Fred Rothenbush '79

THE
SHOOTING

Why You Don't Always Hit What You Shoot At – (Me Too!)

I suppose that most of us who confine our shotgunning to field shooting and the odd warm-up at some clay targets have come to the same conclusion, if we're honest or normal gunners: The highly skilled shotgunner is a very, very rare bird indeed.

So I think we ought to look at several common and unforgiving faults that the occasional shooter has. Learning to eliminate them, one at a time, will make it more likely in the long run for you to understand what <u>you</u> want in a shotgun in terms of fit, balance, choke, etc.

I believe that once you learn a little about the art, whether it's golf or skiing or tennis or shooting, technical talk about the equipment has more meaning. And until you learn why it is that you miss shots you shouldn't, equipment notwithstanding, you can't make much progress in determining just what you want or need in a shotgun.

I assume, and I'm correct probably in most cases, that the gun you're shooting now is something that you're used to and can shoot birds with. I also assume that you have good days and bad without knowing why it is in either case. And, I further assume that on the good days you just don't make as many mistakes. Maybe you have just one of these faults – and if we learn to know what that is, then we're well on the way to that state of grace the old fellows used to enjoy as "being a local legend!"

Upland gunning and waterfowling are, in fact, two distinct types of shooting and we'll take a quick look at each so you'll have something to work on this season.

The duck and goose hunter usually finds the high incomer or the long crossing shot the most mysterious of misses. And so they are – for the simple reason that the longer we have to see and plan a shot, the more time we have to mess it up! The two great mistakes in taking the incomer are these: First, we wait too long trying to "make sure," and second, we "track" the target with a mounted gun – and we commonly make both mistakes with the same shot.

What you want to avoid is trying a relatively vertical shot. It looks easy when the belly of a Canada is right over your head, but everything is against you mechanically, and a bird hit is usually hit too far back. Practice taking the first shot when you think the bird is 45 yards out, do not put the gun to your shoulder until the instant you are going to pull the trigger, take two or three feet of lead and think of shooting into the head. This is really a controlled snap shot. The ideal is to have the bird fall in front of the blind. If the first shot has been a miss or a hit too far back, you still have plenty of time for a good shot long before the target has come to that angle of straight vertical that you really ought to just forget.

Now for a real <u>secret</u>! If the incomer is a bit off the straight line, coming in on the right or left and you're a right-handed shot, <u>give the bird heading right twice as much lead as you do if it crosses to the left</u>! If you think that six feet is enough – double it on the right side and see what happens; and stay with the six feet on the left. Don't ask me to explain it – but I promise you you'll be delighted with the results. Do the same thing on your regular crossing shots as well. But don't put the gun to the shoulder until you're ready to shoot – just follow the flight with the barrel and your hands, keep the stock between the elbow and the shoulder until your mind says <u>now,</u> then go at it. It takes a bit of practice and self-discipline, but it will pay off handsomely in the long run. If you have some flighting doves in your area, that's an ideal time to work on this approach. (And there's no law that says you have to tell everybody your new secret!)

You'll find that not tracking the bird is a hard habit to instill, but try to remember that the longer you swing, the easier it is to slow down or stop. The basic must in all shotgunning is a fast and short swing – one that is accelerating when the trigger is pulled.

The upland gunner doesn't often have the "tracking" problem – he just doesn't have the time. But there is one fault we share here that is close to tracking – and that's trying to make sure, and that's about the last thing that will put a grouse or quail in the game bag.

Before we get into any "secrets," let me tell you that in my opinion the perfect shotgun is one that I'm entirely unconscious of; it is merely a place to put two shells. I don't see barrels, I don't feel a stock – it's part of me, like pointing a finger or, simpler, <u>just looking</u>. And that's the secret here: just looking. As simple as it seems, a vast number of gunners sight down the barrel instead of looking at the bird. Let me assure you, you can't do both and be a good wingshot. You must

95

ignore the gun and look, and look hard, at the target – and wherever your eyes go, the gun barrel will go all by itself! Doesn't that sound easy? It is and it works.

I'd also tell you that it took me a while to learn this and to trust it. It's obvious, when you think about it, that your eyes can't focus on an ivory bead 30 inches away and on a bird 30 yards away at the same time; one has to blur – and the blur has to be the gun barrel. But you have to learn and practice how to look. Let's assume your old setter, Rufus, is on point. The indifferent gunner just walks in, flushes the quail, and maybe grasses a bird or maybe doesn't. But not you! You have made a mental note of the wind direction and the likely course of flight as you walk up, and now, as you expect the flush, be it one bird or 10, your eyes are focused out there at the place where you expect to be shooting the bird – not at your feet! Stare at your target with intensity and concentration – and as in all bird shooting, try to think of shooting at the head. Don't clutter your mind with a lot of intricate arithmetic – stare at the bird and don't mount your gun until the instant you want to shoot. I find it easier to walk in on a point with my gun butt tucked in close between my arm and chest, just under the armpit, rather than in the traditional "port-arms," which involves too much movement and takes a little adjustment for proper gun mounting. And, again, as with any target, if you're a right-handed shooter, lead the left-to-right target more than the right-to-left.

I hope this sounds overly simple to you, since I mean it to; a lot of shooting instruction gets complicated, and what we're trying to do is to eliminate the most common errors. No one is going to take everything he shoots at – or really wants to. But we do want to shoot better and we very much want to eliminate, as much as humanly possible, birds that are body shot and lost, which is why we have to train ourselves to stare at the head and think "head shot" until it becomes automatic. The truly fine shot exhibits an economy of motion and that's a great deal of being precise; the old phrase of "all deliberate speed" is most apt when it comes to handling a shotgun. The biggest reason for any difficulty in learning these little tricks is the elimination of doubt and habit. But the fine gunner is one who has enough of the art in his mind to trust it and then the ability to analyze a miss and see what went wrong; chances are good that he realizes he was either tracking too long or wasn't really looking, staring with concentration, at the bird.

If you have the chance to watch a really top ranked trap or skeet shooter at his game, take note of how far he moves his gun barrel, even at the most extreme angle shot. You'll find that it's rarely more than a foot or so, because he knows that the more you move the gun, the longer you search for the proper lead, the greater the chances of a late and rear-end shot or a miss.

I don't want you to worry about missing, I want you to know that if you follow these simple steps, your shooting will get better; and when you do miss, you'll know why and be able to correct it instantly with the second barrel or on the very next bird. It's not the accumulation of technique that makes a decent field shot – it's the elimination of mistakes.

You can practice a bit at home and it can help a lot. Work on mounting the gun quickly from the ready position of having the stock under the armpit. Carry a gun (leave the shells at home out of season) when you're running the dog in training exercises; not having to worry about shooting does wonders for the nerves, and it gets both the muscles and mind prepared for the real thing. One of the fine British shots I know carries a walking stick and practices with that in downtown London, swinging through pigeons and sparrows, and delights in being looked upon as a harmless eccentric. I can assure you he's anything but harmless to the grouse and pheasant on a downwind drive!

The Main Ingredient

Over the past few years I've read any number of books on shotgun shooting – British and American, amateurs and professionals. All the techniques of lead, swing through, pointing out, sustained lead, "instinct," and variations on these are discussed, propounded, advocated or made light of – depending on what was the common vogue or who claimed to discover a teaching breakthrough.

On top of this, I've been fortunate to have shot with some of our finest gunners, and some just as fine but unknown and unsung. I've attended shooting schools, taken private sessions, and listened in on others being taught. My conclusions? I doubt if anyone can be "taught" to be a shot of the first rank.

You can learn the theories and find the one that suits your temperament and physical equipment best. You can eventually end up with a shotgun that is fitted and balanced to the point of perfection. But there's one critical ingredient that you can't buy or learn – and it's the one that really makes the difference.

It's the ingredient that separates the very good shot, the trap or skeet gunner who gets the odd hundred straight every year, from the many-hundred straight competitor – under the strictest competition – under all kinds of circumstances.

It's the ingredient, and it is still there among a lot of shotgunners, that separated a Kimble or a Bogardus from the other top shots. Since I don't see any reason to separate shooting from the high accomplishments in other sports, the same necessities are needed to create a Ted Williams, a Ty Cobb, a DiMaggio from the many thousands of other baseball players. In any sport, given similar or equal physical ability, a few will always stand out: a few that are really great.

I can, of course, be rightly accused of over-simplification – so you choose the word that seems best to apply: concentration, desire, want-to, willpower…the list could go on, but there's a point here that we'll all appreciate. Given equal equipment and similar physical ability – all men will not post equal scores.

Using Martin Wood's gun, his stance, his ideas, his theories, no doubt I could do a better job at skeet – but not the same job he does. He breaks targets with his mind – his dedication. My dedication is less and my scores reflect it.

The once-popular "instinct" school had school girls hitting pennies in the air with BB guns – as long as the teacher stood behind them and swore that they could do it. He became their dedication – when he left, most of that left with him.

The crux of this is that I believe that the area of greatest skill – and the most difficult to acquire – is this incredible concentration, the concentration that caused Ted Williams to remark that he could "see the stitches on a fast ball." The dedication that makes some great gunners say they see the bird at half-speed – or that the clays look like washtubs.

Can you practice concentration? I think that certain people can. I know I have had the same experience on several occasions, very few, but enough to make me a believer. The modern Chinese government functions, to a large degree, on the political belief that virtually <u>anyone can be taught to do well at anything, with few exceptions</u> if they believe in the need or the duty strong enough. If you are raised on tough heroics, then you can perform them. While I disagree with this both practically and philosophically – I cannot argue that they have strongly proven the premise.

We have been led to believe, in many areas of life, that something new will remove the hurdle of work. Most of us know better. But we continue to buy new guns (no one more guilty of this than I) and find the ultimate magic lacking. Remember the silk purse/sow's ear?

There are some experiments to try that might measure your concentration – and they are fun but not easy. One is to try to break a specific part of a clay target: the front edge, the bottom, or the back. In field shooting, concentrate on the bird's head – you'll forget to shoot for a few – but stick with it if the birds will cooperate. Try to really <u>open your eyes wide</u> – try to see better and clearer – try to slow the bird down; I'll bet you can read the label on a turning 33 rpm record if you concentrate – the trick in shooting is learning to concentrate quickly.

One of the great barriers in trying to teach anyone to shoot is the simple fact that the instructor cannot see what the shooter sees – he does not know exactly what the sight picture was at the moment of firing. And only the most skilled can observe the momentary check of a swing or many of the other brief lapses that cause "unexplainable" misses.

But one thing you can notice is the attitude of the gunner. Is he ready to break the target, is he loafing a little, or is he just so discouraged or indifferent that he'd be better off not shooting at all? The superb shooter is an aggressive shooter. He visibly wants to break that target or bring down that duck.

He's working at it and you can sense it. His body is controlled, his movements are decisive and purposeful. He is a "charger."

One of the difficulties of this kind of aggressive concentration is that you have to learn to control it after you find that you can do it at all. Concentration at this level is quickly exhausting – you have to learn to turn it on and off. I once did a study that showed that an average golfer needed only 12 minutes to play a round of golf making about 90 shots. The rest of the time he's walking around. If you analyze the brief time it's necessary to concentrate on any series of shots – or single periods of time in actual gunning – you'll agree that we ought to be able to improve our dedication a little, since that's all it takes. When the veteran gunner tells the novice that a hundred straight is best taken by thinking one at a time, that's what he's trying to tell him.

Too many of us confuse worry with concentration. Too often we think that being very deliberate is the trick – and of course, we find out that it isn't. The shotgunner has to take a little dare every time; that's the art of it – and the pleasure.

I would say that the most missed shots are the ones that we have a long time to prepare for. The solitary goose swinging in toward the stool from a distance, the cock pheasant seen running ahead of the dog. The fact of spontaneity – the quick reaction – usually produces our best results. The beginning skeet shooter always wonders why he does so well on doubles and misses the easy singles.

Too much mental triangulation, precision – or what have you – wrongly subtracts from the right kind of concentration. Someone once delightfully described walking as a series of interrupted falls. If you tried to monitor every motion required in walking the way we will often do in our shooting, we'd stumble just as badly there too.

The gunner's concentration should be interrupted – at his

control. The vital little rushes of adrenaline we know at the beginning of a match or at the sight of pintails swinging toward the blind is the fuel that our body needs for the next second or so of action. After the shot, relax a little and get rested and get ready, whether you're working quail behind a pointer or in the club championship with your buddies.

Concentration can't be spread over everything you do like paint from a brush. Remember the essentials of shotgun pointing and concentrate on them. The eyes not focused on the sights – but on the area where the bird will be taken.

One superb shooter, Kay Ohye, likes the parallel of weightlifting and shotgunning. The man stands poised over weights – concentrating on getting his adrenaline working, concentrating on how he is going to use this fuel to its best advantage. He knows he can lift it because he's trained his mind as much as his muscles. You know you can do it for the same reasons – he's just gearing up the same way you have to.

We talked before about what you see, actually. This is an area where the average shooter can really help himself by working harder to make his vision more acute. As I said before, he can concentrate, he can physically open his eyes wider to make sure he has the whole possible target area in fine focus. The live-bird shooter will stare at the boxes the pigeon is going to come from, mount his gun, make sure he sees all the traps and that his eyes are sharp – if things get a little blurry, he'll take his gun down and start over. The quail hunter who spends all day watching his feet isn't going to do as well as the one who spends his time looking at the area out in front of the dog.

When you're watching "out there," you are aware of wind, light, shadow – and you program the possibilities. You get an idea of the bird's speed, the altitude, and you're subconsciously fixing yourself to do the right gun pointing before the gun comes to your shoulder because you know that the quicker you shoot after the butt hits your shoulder, the better your chances – don't second guess yourself – and you don't have to rush because you've already studied out most of the possibilities. Sure we'll get fooled or overconfident, everyone does, but these are the kind of mistakes that we learn from – not the "misses that are mysteries."

"Aim High, Keep the Gun Moving, and Never Check"

As a rather passionate book collector, especially when the material has anything to do with shotguns, I can honestly say that if there's a theory about wingshooting, I'm sure I've read it. Further, in order to learn – and with the seemingly vain hope of self-improvement – I've spent some time at the Purdey Shooting Grounds and a few other such places and have plans to attend others. I have been coached at both skeet and trap by some outstanding champions and have been lucky to have been in the hunting field with a few of these "legends." First of all, I can gladly assure you that they can miss just like the rest of us; not always for the same reason or as often.

In general, field shooting is not, for most of us and rightly so, a competitive situation. We all like to do well, but not much more than a funny dinnertime story or two is really at stake. Most of us can't bring to bear the fine edge of

105

concentration needed to perform at a near-perfect level. And we don't shoot enough, practice enough, or ever dry-fire enough to attain a high level of familiarity with our guns or even decent muscle memory. We're weekend gunners at best, and not nearly enough of that.

Now, since I am for these moments acting as the "small end of the funnel," what have I learned that I can pass on that might be of some help? I have to assume that your gun fits pretty well – and I can assure you that it doesn't have to be perfect as long as it doesn't throw the charge a foot or so off from where it should. I further assume that you can see fairly well and that your reflexes are good enough so that you aren't continually slamming the car door on your fingers.

If we're still together at this point, I will use the advice of Lord Ripon, who was, without question, about the greatest game shot that ever lived. His Honorable Self tells us: "Aim high, keep the gun moving, and never check." That's all there is to it.

Ripon assumes, and correctly, that we have instantly calculated range, speed of flight, and whatever angles are functional. These little niceties come with experience, but given a little of that – at least enough to keep us from raw panic at the flush of a bird or the passing of a flock of downwind teal – we ought to be able to keep the gun moving and not check. Right? Maybe...

Ripon assumes, which is his privilege as it was his habit, that we concentrate on the task at hand. And most of us will do better on the unexpected or quite difficult shot than we will on the routine. The beginner at skeet always does better on his doubles than he does on his singles because he doesn't have time to carefully "measure" and just goes ahead and swings without checking.

Ripon also assumes that we don't make the basic mistakes

Fred Rothenbush

of looking down the barrel and focusing on the sights or having a too-heavy or too-light trigger pull or shooting a gun and shell combination that hurts us and makes us flinch, or any of a number of other things that are ancient history to the very skillful shooter. Shooters who "check" their swing, that is, pause or stop, do so out of uncertainty – mechanical or mental – that interrupts the decision just made.

The Ripons of the shooting world have very few uncertainties. They know that every shot, every swing, isn't necessarily perfect – and that it needn't be – it just has to be good enough so that the ordinary pattern that is almost 15 feet long and about 30 inches wide will have intercepted the target. They know that being too precise is one of the great faults of the ordinary gunner – or at least his trying to be; he thinks too much and then questions his judgment – and checks!

On one of my shelves of shooting books, there is a bit or two about Lord Ripon you might find interesting: "The legend of Lord Ripon rests simply on the fact that he could kill more birds than anybody else. He himself liked to pretend that his skill was achieved effortlessly and he once wrote, 'Practice makes perfect, in the case of shooting, is true only to a certain extent, for a man must be born with a certain inherent aptitude to become a really first-rate shot.' In whatever way he achieved it, success certainly came to him; there was nobody his equal. He once killed twenty-eight pheasants in a minute. On another occasion he shot so quickly and accurately that he had seven dead birds in the air at once."

Of course, Ripon was shooting with a pair of guns – sometimes a trio – and using a loader as was the custom. I believe his favorite guns were outside-hammer Purdeys. They are also a favorite of mine, but there I'm afraid the comparison ends.

Much that has been written about the art of shooting, including my own efforts, can be confusing. Too often, we say one thing and do another, and at the bottom it has always been my contention that the best teacher is a case of shells, maybe two.

In reality, Ripon was a tireless "practicer." At a weekend of shooting, he was careful to avoid too much food and wine and did his best to get a decent amount of rest – not an easy formula to follow in the heyday of the lavish shooting parties that often included masquerade balls or other entertainments. I am a great believer in gun handling and keep one or two handy before and during the shooting season and spend a couple of minutes dry pointing several times a day. My dreams of being a legend are long-since forgotten, but I am an advocate of "every bit helps."

One of the concepts of practice or even thinking about wingshooting is it helps remove doubt or indecision: "checking." And developing familiarity with your gun is a good way to start. Take an empty gun along when you walk the dog – whatever, but get into the habit of handling it often before opening day.

I'm sure when the story got out about Ripon lying on his back in the summer shooting at dragonflies with a .410, he was in for some strange looks. But, here was a man who had no off season and the looks were different when he left his stand in the field. He was truly the envy of kings.

I am delighted to say that nowhere in his discourses on shooting does Lord Ripon indulge in the common absurdity of "a pheasant flying at 40 mph at 30 yards should be led by six feet," or some other such nonsense. I firmly believe that such arithmetic has retarded the shooting ability of most of us as much or more than anything that claimed to be scientific advice.

Numbers are interesting, such as 38-24-36 proves to be, but not in shooting lessons. It is the speed of <u>your</u> reactions and

<u>your</u> swing that determines <u>your</u> leads – not mine.

Here I remind you of another great line about shooting: "Don't think – shoot!" I seriously doubt if Ripon ever read anything about shooting on the wing. It doesn't seem to have affected his ability – and I have a feeling that the little he himself wrote about it was done with some reluctance in the firm belief that it was a very poor substitute for a gun in the hands and a couple of pockets full of cartridges – and an inquiring mind.

By now, I feel like the "scholar" who has done a 40-page thesis on a 14-line sonnet; it's been fun and educational for me, and perhaps you might find something to take home, as the old saying goes.

In Lord Ripon's time (1867-1923), it was a common custom to keep a personal shooting diary. In it, he listed both the number and species of game. For the year 1889, the total, including a few hares, rabbits, and one or two deer, came to 18,239. When he finally tired of records in 1923, his grand total came to 556,813. Think about that for a minute, then remember: "Aim high, keep the gun moving, and never check."

Getting
the
Range

I'm often surprised at how often a shooter who is relatively experienced seems to have only the most rudimentary idea of distance. This was brought home to me in an exaggerated way last year when I was shooting driven pheasant in Yorkshire.

I was standing at my place in line at the edge of a lake, and two birds flew over well to my left – and the gun well to my right fired twice. I turned to see what he could have been shooting at since I'd only seen those two birds and they were a minimum of 80 yards from him. But then the drive began in earnest; I discovered that the man was now shooting at birds crossing in front of him at the other side of the lake, 70 or 80 yards away. Needless to say, nothing fell.

When the drive was over, I went to where he was standing and heard him say that he would have to go back to shooting school or get a new pair of guns. I asked what he was shooting and he handed me one of a pair of truly magnificent William Evans, sidelock ejector game guns of the first rank, with the quality of a Holland or Purdey but without the long reputation

– or the high price – but the Evans didn't come exactly for box tops either.

I admired the guns and asked one of his friends if he had seen what I had – an afternoon of impossible distances. He said he had and that the man always did that, and that the only time he shot at all well was when the birds didn't appear until they were in range and that he'd been told and shown countless times what was within range and what wasn't, but nothing "took."

This is an extreme example, the worst I've seen this side of some buckshot-using goose hunters who have ruined a few of my days in Maryland and Delaware. But the inability to judge range is anything but rare and about equally mixed with gunners who won't shoot at anything farther than 35 yards and those who seem to think that if they can see it and can get far enough in front of it, they can bring it down.

What little research exists in this area indicates that the greatest errors are in the critical line of 50 yards; too many shotgunners think that 65 is really 50 and too many think that they can ordinarily take birds at these ranges: <u>wrong</u>!!

Of course, we've all seen birds killed at 50, 55, and 60 yards and rarely even a bit farther. But we've never seen it done regularly and we never will and not because it's impossible to establish the correct lead either, but because the laws of physics are against us. The statistics themselves aren't all that interesting, but you can take my word for it that the efficiency line of a full choke shotgun, perfectly matched with the shell it shoots best, using a heavy load of 4's or 5's, is drawn at 50 yards. Or ought to be! For steel shot, no matter the load, 45 yards is just plain <u>it</u>.

The most difficult distance to judge is vertical – straight up. I've suggested to several waterfowl camps that they put up a balloon that's 40 yards high – put it up against the tallest tree

around and let the shooters see the point of reference. It's not rare to see a gunner pass up a shot that's just over treetop height – and it's a very tall tree indeed that's 100 feet – but make no hesitation at all to shoot at something half again as far when it's off at a lesser angle rather than straight up.

One good habit is to pace off distances, after guessing at them, when you're out for a walk with the dog. You'll be surprised, too, at how the degree of light makes things seem close or far. Another is to pace off yardage when you leave a blind to retrieve a bird or pick one up in a field. It doesn't take much practice to improve, but it does take a little restraint not to shoot when you're in doubt.

In my own case, a 50-yard shot has to be perfect for me to chance it; I'll take a straight incomer, but turn down a right-angle crossing bird in favor of a crossing shot that is getting closer. In brief, I am not gunning to prove my shooting ability in difficult situations, but to take a few birds for the table under circumstances where I am most apt to kill cleanly. A better shot or one more used to extreme angles might decide otherwise.

I might, at first, refuse a few long-flushing quail or pheasant and then when I've adjusted to the birds and cover, decide that I can handle them. But I would far rather leave the field with a little kidding about my "cherry picking" than I would with the knowledge that I'd hit birds that we couldn't recover. I know I'm not the best dove shot in the world because I've been fortunate enough to gun with a couple of men who are by far my better. They will take and execute shots that I refuse. But when the day is over, my average will be close to theirs. I've learned both distances and my personal limitations. Some days they will go out in the dove field and shoot 12 gauge, full choke guns and take nothing but 40 to 45 yard shots. I'll shoot next to them with my open-bored 28 gauge and take nothing over 35 yards – in reality we're doing the same thing, using our guns and skills to their potential.

In the upland bird field, working with dogs, I try to make a fast estimate of my field of fire – a tree or bush will establish my 40-yard limit or less, depending on the thickness of the cover and what gun I'm using, and when I doubt about whether it's my shot or my partner's, I try to favor him, knowing that he will usually do the same for me.

What we've been thinking about is, at bottom, sportsmanship. Part of the definition, at least in my mind, is deciding at a critical moment whether to do something or not – whether it's chancing a shot at a bird that might be a bit stretchy or taking a quail that might be a touch closer to someone else; deciding, "What the hell," or saying, "Wait a minute."

I'm always pleased, as are all of us, to see someone shoot well, but even more pleased to see someone allow the right thing to happen even though in our times of few chances and little opportunities, it is growing more and more difficult to stand there and do nothing – often the most positive act we can manage in the field.

Having a good retriever is no excuse for having a day filled with sailing ducks and geese or anything else. Making one of those 65-yard shots is no excuse for thinking that skill had anything to do with it.

Some Federal areas limit the amount of ammunition you can take in the blind in an effort to make the gunner into a more deliberate person – a little harsh, but it seems to work. It wouldn't be a bad idea for each of us to do the same thing. If your limit of geese is four, you ought to be able to handle that well inside a box of shells even if you are completely out of practice. If you're a decent shot, two or three shells per bird is ample. If you use up your allotment and fall short of the limit, you ought to have learned something: Either your gun doesn't fit, you're not using the basic principles of shooting, or you are shooting at birds out of range – the first two are a little embarrassing; the last is inhumane and cruel.

The next time you see someone "chance" a shot at a bird smart enough to be out of range, and you see the bird hurt and set his wings to drift away, I hope you take a minute to imagine what the bird will be going through for the little while it will probably live – and I hope you'll be thankful that you're not the sort of person who would cause something like that to happen.

Of Pheasant
and Things

Years ago when I was foolish enough to consider myself a
dog trainer, I did a lot of bird gunning under severe
conditions, the kind of long-range shots that you would
ordinarily think about twice. At the same time I did a fair
amount of gunning for retriever field trials, not ideal either.
Most of the birds were pheasants and most of those were
heavy, lumbering fliers not all that hard to hit but capable of
absorbing a lot of pellet energy and difficult to take cleanly.

After a little experimentation and a lot of good advice from
more experienced gunners, I ended up using an old trap gun of
mine, an over-under that threw close to full choke patterns
from both barrels and shot a little high. It was a little heavy
and slow, but speed wasn't the problem – results were. The
field trial judges wanted birds <u>dead</u> and not under your
feet either, and I wanted the same thing when I was working
my own Labs.

We all preach patterning and rightly so, but that's only part
of field shooting for large and heavy birds. We also know the
theory of the multiple effect of small shot, 7½'s and 8's, and
the likelihood of lethal hits increased with an increase in shot

number. And while all this sounds good, shotgunning is a compromise. What none of the paper shows is the ability of a bird to absorb transferred energy, and since we really don't know all the answers, we have to rely in part on observation and common sense.

Very few shotguns are either perfect or terrible with most shot sizes, but we know that open barrels pattern small shot better than they do large sizes. We also know that the most famous barrel makers, Dan Lefever and Burt Becker to name a couple of legends, preferred to make tight chokes and work with the shot in sizes 4, 5, and 6, believing as I do that for ducks and pheasants you are best prepared when you are ready for the worst.

My own pheasant loads ended up being 3¼ dram with 1¼ ounces of either 5's or 6's, 12 gauge of course. These put the birds where I wanted them and did it cleanly as long as I did my part. No shell and gun combination can make you into a Fred Kimble, but if you're not in that class of gun pointer, you sure want everything else going for you. A pheasant or duck, especially in the late part of the season, is a heavy and well-feathered and fleshed bird. You need shot of some size and velocity to achieve lethal penetration and minimize crippling. I have taken a lot of both birds with 7½'s, but I'm convinced beyond all argument that this is not a good load beyond 30 yards, and not nearly as potent as either the 5's or 6's at any yardage. There are no statistics on the tenacity of life for birds either, but I rank the duck and pheasant at the top as will anyone who has done much gunning for either. I believe it's wrong to pursue either bird species with less than the maximum efficiency of both gun and shell. And I'll add on a good gun dog for good measure!

The British are the real experts on pheasant shooting and, although most of their birds are shot as driven incomers, they have most thoroughly studied what works and why. The load of choice there is a size 6, and while somewhat smaller than our 6, it works for the same reasons – size and transference of energy at moderate to extreme ranges. I prefer our heavier loading in this country for the simple reasons that most of our birds are going away, presenting a less vulnerable target area, and most of their birds are taken from underneath at often closer yardages.

I also mentioned that I like a gun that shoots a bit high. One of the most common faults of the shotgunner is deliberate aiming. This means that the shooter is not focusing on the bird but looking too strongly at his barrel; the result is often a low shot and even when a bird is so hit the chances are that the shot will strike the belly area, resulting in a lot of feathers but leaving a crippled bird with plenty of strength for flight. An old verse on pheasants says:

"Should Pheasant rise, be most particular –
He rises nearly perpendicular."

I know too well that it's easier said than done, but take a second to see your target and make a conscious effort for a head shot. I promise you, you won't shoot over many and you'll have fewer body-hit birds that you'll either lose or have to run down. If you're unfortunate enough to be in a steel shot area, the choice of choke will be modified and if you get any kind of decent pattern with big shot – as big as 4's, I'd try those; but be prepared to shoot twice, as steel, in my experience, does not carry the knock-down power of lead.

Lessons
from
Doves

I write about shooting doves with the same compulsion that must have driven the climbers of Everest and caused the early Christian monks to flog themselves with sticks: It's difficult and painful, but something makes me do it.

But there has never been a season that opening day didn't find me fresh with theories and confident of that achievement that ranks with going four-for-four, the hat trick, or par out, par in: a limit of 20 with a few shells left over in the box. But as it usually turns out, I end up batting about .287, no goals, and barely breaking 90.

Why? Is it that I have no idea of how to point a shotgun? not entirely. Is it that I cannot risk trying something bizarre? Sometimes. Is it that the dove is often too much for me to handle? Now and then. But, like most of us, it seems on reflection that the dove is too subtle for us too often. The dove is like those little quarter angles at trap: We are so confident that we <u>know</u>, when in fact we don't, until it's too late.

If I were standing behind you, calling your shots, a gun far removed from my hand, I would say, "This one looks like an incomer, but it really is sliding a bit to your left," and you would shift your shoulders slightly, follow the bird with the tip of the barrel – the gun not fully mounted, then with one smooth stroke, tuck the butt into your shoulder and pull the trigger. We would then have the satisfaction of adding another morsel to the evening meal. On a left-to-right crosser, I would say, "Steady, lad, this is not just as it seems. The dove is, in actuality, going more than a bit away and is climbing a touch" – so you would reduce the lead you'd first factored in, adjust for a higher angle and, just as you shot, you'd smile with satisfaction.

Perhaps you could do this all by yourself – no doubt you have, and so have I – but not as often as we should. We daydream and wish that the shot will be one of those that we are almost always sure of – and shoot <u>there</u>, not where the dove actually is – or will be in a split second.

The point of this is to remind you of a couple of wingshooting's most common faults, one of which is <u>not really looking at the target</u>. It is said that certain shooters can see the individual feathers, or the brightness of the eye – and I am a believer. I also believe that so can we, enough so that if we concentrated on trying, our bird/shell ratio would improve markedly. But, like a downhill two-foot putt, it is a lot harder than it looks. It takes practice.

Not long ago, I was visiting with one of the all-time great trapshooters. It was a cold and dismal mid-winter afternoon and I found him in his cellar punching a tennis ball that hung from the ceiling by a string. "What are you up to?" I asked him. "Working on my hand-eye coordination," he told me. "I do it almost every day for a few minutes. It's to the shooter what sparring is to the fighter." An expert shot as well as an inexpert one have one thing in common – no time, or not much, to think. You have to rely on reflexes. If they're honed by training and practice – marvelous. If they're our usual "let's throw one out there somewhere and hope," we're not going to do as well as we'd like.

I realize that practicing shooting, other than by burning up shells, seems silly to most of us. A lot of us simply don't care that much. But for those of us who do or are in a slump – as I am at this writing – it makes a little sense to think about it. Even the very best golfers take lessons constantly and practice incessantly. Why do 99 out of 100 shooters believe that the Almighty gave them an athletic skill He didn't give anyone else? I can't answer that question either, since I'm more than a little guilty myself – and my scores reflect it.

But there are some simple checks on your form that are absurdly easy, so why not try them? I learned them at an English shooting school and they're common to many teachers. To practice on the high incomer, stand under a telephone wire and bring your gun along the wire until the barrels are straight overhead. If you do it quickly, you might find that you're favoring one side or another. If you do this consistently, close one eye a little (the left eye if you're right-handed) and see if that keeps you straight along the line. What often happens on this bird, if you miss it, is that you subconsciously move the barrel off to one side to see the bird. In truth, this is the one shot that you'll often make where you can't see the target if you do it right at certain angles. You can do the same thing in reverse for going-away birds.

Lest you think you'll feel silly, my famous trapshooter friend does about the same thing – and he does it almost every day. Across one wall in his workshop is a map of target angles laid out with duct tape: straightaways, acute left and right angles, and so on. And almost every day he mounts his gun and "shoots" for half an hour.

One of the great attractions about doves is that you get to shoot a lot, and the dove field is where you sharpen up for the coming waterfowl season, the quail season, or whatever – but here is where you can <u>work</u> on gun pointing. It's a shame to waste the chance by just going out and donating 10 percent of your income to the ammunition companies. Study your shots, learn to look at the bird and, if you can, have someone stand behind you and double check what you're doing wrong – or, it is hoped, right.

Learning to Use the Second Shot

One of the measures of a good shot in the field is how well he can use the second shot. (I never put three shots into a pump or auto unless I'm hunting waterfowl. From a practical point, the third shot is rarely functional.)

The traditional British theory is that a double barrel is designed to take <u>two birds</u>. If you miss with the first, the second is used for another bird – the first bird, having escaped, is merely given your best wishes for a long life.

That may be fine when you're shooting driven birds in Scotland where you'll get more shots in a single day than most of us take all season, but I don't feel it applies to "walk-up" or pass shooting.

In the excitement or surprise of a flushed bird or a downwind broadbill, our first shot is too often "by fright, not sight." Then we can calm down a hair and do the job with the next shell. Maybe.

Here's what happens when the second shot goes as awry as the first: Recoil has jarred our face away from the stock, and the gun is fired as soon as we pull it back into place, or maybe a bit sooner. Result – two shots in the same empty space.

We can also swing the head around but not bring the barrel along with it. Or we leave the head off the stock entirely and shoot under or over the bird. So:

Don't panic: Just settle down, take the time to be precise. Never let your eyes leave the bird.

Hold the gun a little tighter in your hands and against your shoulder, as a matter of course, on every shot.

Get the head down on the stock – and take a little more lead for the increased distance on a going-away or crossing bird.

Getting mentally and physically ready for a second shot will surely improve your first barrel as well in a little time.

Shoot some clay targets, and use the second shot on the big piece when you break it on the first shot.

Stay with the target with your eyes – even if it's his – and on big birds like geese don't hesitate to shoot again. (I've almost never seen a big duck, wild pheasant, or goose that was useless because it was shot up.)

I've seen some very fine shots in the live-pigeon ring get periods where they miss bird after bird with the first barrel and bring it down with the second because they are prepared to shoot twice every time. Shooting the second barrel will require thought. It must be treated as a separate shot, not a repeat of the first. The British shooting schools teach taking the gun off the shoulder between shots, remounting it, and then shooting. Not a bad procedure for the field shooter to try if he has first-barrel problems.

The Art
of
Shooting Quail

At bottom, quail shooting isn't really any different than most other birds that are totally frustrating, heart-stopping at the flush, seem to instinctively know which is your "bad" side, and where the nearest thick brush is. The only real "expert" advice I can offer is to not go gunning quail if you're easily upset about being embarrassed in front of your friends and/or bird dogs. And, just one more bit – don't brag about what you did last time out or in the least way hint that you have any more than the most rudimentary knowledge of shotgunning.

The one thing that seems to set quail outings apart from most other bird hunts is the necessity and the tradition of manners – both in the gunners and the bird dogs. If there is a sport where it's "not how many, but how," it's gunning quail.

The "Gentleman's Quail Gun" has long been considered the 20. And why argue about it? Even in the autoloaders, the weight of the little gun is an acceptable less-than-seven-pounds; that's more than it should weigh, but the American gunmaker has never concerned himself with such niceties. It's always struck me as odd that in Britain and Europe where a person shoots a lot and carries very little, gun balance and weight are essential criteria of quality, and here, where the reverse is true, most of our guns are made as if one of their primary functions is jacking up wagons. Of course our gunmakers had their theories too, but lying not too deep behind them was the idea that they'd be damned if they'd copy such fancy ideas from England; and they surely didn't.

So having decided that we are gentlemen and will shoot the 20 gauge, what should be the choke? I would guess that about eight out of 10 quail guns that are single barreled – pumps and autos – are bored improved cylinder, as they should be. But suppose fortune has smiled on us and we want to do it up right with an over-under or side-by-side; what now?

Well, now we will probably start an argument – but hear me out. I would suggest that you consider the old standard game boring of improved cylinder – or even <u>pure cylinder</u> – and make the second barrel improved modified. Now before you jump up and spill your drink, think back on the <u>majority</u> of second shots you've had on a covey or even a single. Think of the cover where you do most of your gunning, think of windy days late in the season, think of the odd bird dog that is a little less than perfect, and think of having an extra second or two if you want it. And think of the fact that you're using, in most cases, less than an ounce of shot.

I went through the same dilemma with a cylinder and full bird gun. From the first, I swore I'd have the second barrel opened up, but in the course of two or three years, I kept some sort of sloppy record of where I was really reaching for the bird with the second barrel, and it ended up at close to 30 yards, maybe a little more.

But what really convinced me to leave it alone was the knowledge that I didn't have to rush (or throw away)

the second barrel, and I must say that I did rather well with it. Most of us are not as fast as we wish we were anyway, so I don't see any reason to pay a penalty when it isn't necessary.

Not to dwell on it any more than need be, but I suggest you pattern some 20's, those of your friends or whatever, and do it at 35 yards with your bird load of 8's or 7½'s. If you don't have confidence in a gun, you really won't do well with it; that's always been a valid reason for me to at least do a few patterns on paper; it's usually reassuring that if you point it where it belongs, it will do just what it should.

While we're on that idea of having a gun that is perfect, I'd like mine to shoot about half a pattern, 12-15 inches, high at 35-40 yards. And I would just as soon have double triggers – I'm surprised at how often I do select the choke barrel by using the back trigger and how seldom (or never) have I ever seen anyone do so with a single selective trigger.

The best quail load? I'll stay with 8's or 7½'s. It really doesn't make much difference unless it's very cold or you have to reach a little more, and then 7½'s get the nod. I wouldn't bother with the 3-inch shell since I personally don't like the recoil or the price. In the long run, it isn't that much more effective.

If there is any secret to being a good quail shot, part of it has to be in knowing how to position yourself. By that I mean both paying attention to where the birds are most likely to fly when flushed and then pointing your left foot (if all goes well) at the most difficult angle that is likely to be offered so you'll be able to make a full swing without losing your balance. I would suggest you practice the technique of coming in on the dogs with the butt of the gun tucked lightly in your armpit or just in front of it. This will give you one easy and short move to a proper gun mount. If there is a more common or worse way to bring up a shotgun than from the port-arms carry, I don't know of it. I suspect that all that gun-waving around, which is unnecessary, is the cause of more misses than any other single thing. Why make it all harder than it has to be?

And to be on the safe side, I will repeat what I've written a million times: Do not look at the gun barrel or the sight – look only at the bird and trust your instincts to swing through: <u>Don't aim</u>!!

Please watch your own bird when you shoot. Look for a leg down, watch for a sudden pitching and mark it as best you can. If you have a dog that retrieves, let it get in where the bird is before you thrash all over the cover. Use your eyes first and your feet last. If you shoot two birds, you still have to mark them down. It's a habit you ought to have and not rely on someone else; part of the good manners we talked about earlier.

Let's assume that a dog is on point and you're walking in to shoot. What's the first thing on your mind? To make sure where everyone else is! If you have a partner walking in with you, make sure he has his half of the firing field – don't worry overly about a bird getting away; no one will remember that as much as they'll remember you shooting a bird that really belonged to someone else. Be careful of young dogs – they too often will leap for a flushed bird or chase after a low flyer. If you have any questions, don't be reluctant to ask the dog handler. I have seen, far too often, a shooter so hesitant about coming in behind a dog on point that he almost forces the dog to break – when you walk in to flush birds, do it boldly, don't make the birds run or the dog check; if you wonder about doing it right – ask.

And unless they're your dogs, leave them alone. Don't ever work another man's dog, and it ought to go without saying – don't criticize it, either.

At the end of a day gunning quail, the summing up ought to center around having a good day rather than a filled limit.

Good manners, unceasing care about safety, and the pleasure of the dogs come first. The act of hunting quail as well as the bird itself demand thought and care. Being a good shot is not nearly as important as being a good companion.

Notes
on
Shotshells

A famous architect once made the provocative remark that "less is more," a statement that has been studiously ignored by the shotshell manufacturers of this country – to their profit.

In my opinion, the shotgunning market of America has been dominated by the "needs" of the waterfowler. It was this market that eagerly wanted "Hi-Power" and "Hi-Velocity" and "Magnums." And as long as they were willing to pay the premium, they got them. But so did the rest of us, whether we wanted them or not.

Another factor in the leap to artillery-sized charges was the fact that the duck hunter also fell in love with the autoloading shotgun; here was firepower that he could, and did, come to grips with until the Feds limited him to three shots, but by that time the autoloader was as American as the Fourth of July – and for similar reasons. And in order to make this contraption work when it was cold and overoiled and undercleaned, you supplied a shell that supplied enough recoil to move a mule or a gunner who thought like one.

But the truth is often not what it seems to be, nor what we want it to be. In shotgun shells, more is often less. To begin, we know that about five pellets of properly sized shot (in proportion to the size of the quarry) are generally lethal. We also know that it's not the number of shot in the shell that really counts, but the number of shot in our 30-inch circle at about 35 yards that bags the most birds.

I'm going to skip over duck and goose loads since they've been complicated by the mandate of steel shot. What this preacher wants you to consider – hopefully to your benefit – is the use of light loads for upland gunning.

By "light," I mean the new one ounce or 1⅛ ounce 12-gauge shells that have been produced for the trap and skeet shooters; and not the bizarre 3¼ dram-equivalent with one ounce of shot – but the standard 2¾ dram. Maybe even the light 2½-inch shells from Britain now more readily available in this country.

Why? Well, for one thing they're extraordinarily pleasant to use and, for another, surprisingly effective. If your gun is going to hurt you when you pull the trigger, you aren't going to use it to the best of your wingshooting capabilities. And by "light" I mean the ⅞-ounce load in the 20 and the ¾-ounce load in the 28 gauge. For those smart enough to have held onto their 16's, the one-ounce load is ideal for that as well.,

Not being a physicist, and assuming that most of you aren't either, you'll have to trust me when I tell you that a one-ounce load will often pattern better at normal game ranges (25 to 35 yards) than will heavier loadings, and this will hold true with the light loadings in the other gauges as well. There's a magical balance between bore diameter and the shot mass that produces this splendid result. I apologize for using the non-technical "magical," but even the much more learned ballisticians can't give you the proof in numbers, and who cares as long as the results are what we want?

If you see the gun barrel as a funnel and can imagine pouring X amount of shot through it, you can quickly see that a smaller amount of shot will pass through faster, resulting in a shorter shot string, which is the critical factor in the surprising effectiveness of small amounts of shot: Most of the shot arrives at the same place at the same time! The low pressure required to throw a small amount of shot means there will be less pellet deformation as well as less recoil, nudging your shotgun variables toward the ideal.

Leaving this learned discussion in favor of the dove or quail field, I will bet my cooler against yours that if you avoid the one ounce 20-bore load and stay with the lighter one, you will bag more. My shooting has proven to me that a light 20-gauge shotgun kicks me into sloppy shooting after a short time; I begin to anticipate recoil and do odd things with the gun instead of smoothly swinging through the bird.

I am six feet tall and run about 190 and will freely admit to being recoil-shy; most gunners are whether they admit it or not or even think about it. And I will apply this to using an autoloader even though its recoil effect is somewhat less. In case you're interested, my guns of choice for quail are either my 12 gauge using a one-ounce load or a 28 with the ¾-ounce load – depending on whim and how wild I guess the birds will be or the density of the cover and how far I think my average shot will be and how much time I will have to make it. If you're still interested, and this is an important factor, my 12 weighs a shade over 6½ pounds, and the 28 right at 5½.

What the light loads allow us to do is match the load to both the size of the bird and the weight of the gun, and since upland birds are small and vulnerable, what we need is evenness of pattern at normal game ranges, not an excess of pellets stringing out all over Creation where they add nothing to the effectiveness of our gun. The only limitations with these light loads is distance, and that is largely a function of choke rather than the amount of the load of shot. It's the rare shot that is over 25 yards, so why pattern your bird gun at 40? I suggest that 30 to 32 yards be your standard, easily proved by pacing off the next few birds you down in the field.

I wish I could say that another great advantage is that light loads are less expensive, but unhappily that isn't the case. Apparently ammunition companies believe that when it comes to profit, "less is more."

But try a box or so of the lightest loads you can find for your game gun – see if you don't shoot a little better.

The Myth
of Speed

Some years ago when I was interested in tournament skeet shooting, I had the opportunity to watch a shootoff between an old-time crusader and a young and promising star. The youngster was dramatic and awesome as he obliterated targets almost before I could see them come out of the house. The older man, I seem to recall that he was well over 60, was nerve-wracking to watch as he rode every target until the last possible instant, and several seemed only inches from the ground before he broke them.

Of course you can guess what happened: The slower Chet shot, the faster the kid had to be, and it was only a matter of time until brains and ego clashed and a high-6 target just kept on going as if it didn't know how good the eyes and reflexes of a 20-year-old can be.

In the international "flyer" or live-pigeon competition, in my opinion the supreme test of shotgunning skills, the spectators are often dazzled by the almost incredible speed of some of the youngsters who sometimes drop a bird within a couple of feet of the traps. But when the races are over and the winners march to the podium for their medals, as often as not the ribbons are slipped over a thatch of graying hair.

I don't mean to imply that shooting, either field or competitive, is a matter of the "tortoise and the hare," but while speed is a factor to one degree or another, it is not, by any means, the <u>decisive</u> factor. Give me the man with judgment and experience every time.

It's no secret that after we reach the age of 40, most of us have lost a bit of visual acuity and are slower in our reflexes. But "slow" is a very relative term. I believe that even well into the 70's or beyond, our ability to mount a gun, make the necessary allotment of lead, etc., is well within the parameters of a satisfying and successful day in the field. I often shoot against several men who are right around the octogenarian era who never fail to turn in very creditable performances.

To paraphrase the old golf saying of, "It's not how, but how many," we know that in shooting it's not how fast, but how accurate. And there are some adjustments we have to make as we get less nimble of foot and all that goes with it. But, these are not at all difficult – once we have the common sense to admit that the eye-hand coordination needs a little more assist from the brain.

First, I assume that you have a pair of <u>shooting</u> glasses made in your prescription. If you don't, you should, and I'd suggest a very light tinted brown or amber as a good compromise color. Second, to avoid unnecessary fatigue, take a little time to shed the excess weight in your equipment. There are several new types of hunting boots that incorporate synthetic fabrics that can add miles to your day or energy to the miles. Also, take fewer shells. I've discovered that using a shell belt instead of stuffing your pockets with ammunition takes a lot of weight off your shoulders and makes it easier to weave your way through brush. Simply put, lay your stuff out and if you can do without it, leave it home.

The older and experienced gunner doesn't have to take too

many unnecessary steps. He waits a few minutes and studies a bird field before he sends the dogs in. He checks the wind, looks for the likely spots, and takes his time. In my careless youth, I literally ruined a couple of bird dogs because I was determined to cover as much ground as I could, and I pushed my dogs into an absurdly fast pace. All they were concerned about was staying in front of me and that meant more running than hunting. I know better now, but I still wonder at the hard-headedness of my attitude and the total lack of common sense.

You might even consider one of the leather gun slings with a loop that fits over the barrel and another that fits over the stock; you can use it for carrying when you want and slip it off the gun when you want – it will surely help keep your arms from getting too tired, and it's a great help on those walks to the blinds when you're out for waterfowl.

I'd suggest trying to borrow a lighter gun and see how you do with it before making the investment or trading away a gun that you've shot well for years. There is an old saying that I've adapted to my shotgunning on a broad basis and that's, "Don't fix anything until it's broke."

If it comes down to taking fewer shots and still hitting them as opposed to burning a little more powder with sketchy results, I'd opt for the gun that puts the birds in the game pocket.

There are pitifully few things I remember from my years of high school, but there's one Latin phrase that applies to this theme: festina lentex – make haste slowly. I think we tend to worry unduly about being slower or less precise when, in fact, taking a bit more time in getting to the field or blind, hunting, and the critical act of shooting itself will prove to be a positive factor instead of the reverse.

Gunning shouldn't be an endurance contest, nor is there any law that I know of that says you have to grass a bird before it has its legs tucked up for flight. The only real bottom line is that you have an enjoyable day. Sit and smoke your pipe, take a look at the countryside, give the dogs a breather. Now's the time to utilize your woods sense, your experience of when and where a bird will fly, and be ready with the calmness of knowing that you have the skill to take your game cleanly.

I don't walk as many miles as I used to, but I do take more birds with fewer shots. I know what I can do and what I can't, what my dogs will do and what they won't. I know when I can take a duck or goose and when to let them pass by. I'm always out there when I can be. I don't have anything against being young – but then I don't have anything against the skills of a Rudy Etchen, either!

While this has been addressed to the 40-plus gunner, there isn't any reason why anyone who is conscious of rushing his shooting, who gets a little panicked at the flush of a bird or the approach of waterfowl to the decoys, can't remember to practice taking it a little easy. Take a split second or longer to rehearse your skills, visualize what you want to do; run a mini-motion picture in your brain – and then do it. This little "rehearsal" just before you go into action is a marvelous habit and well worth working on because it gives you something positive to focus on when you see a dog on point or birds working toward your blind.

All of us are guilty of making wingshooting more difficult than it is. We worry too much about missing then subconsciously rush to get the whole thing over with. That is a negative approach and is self-destructive to success. Remember the good shots and how you made them and accept the misses as part of your personal learning program.

Taking a little more time allows you to do the few things that are vital to good shooting. <u>Concentrate</u> on seeing the bird, not just shooting in the general direction; <u>do not</u> mount the gun until you are ready to shoot, and then fire the instant the butt touches your shoulder – do not track the target, since this is the greatest single cause of stopping the gun or slowing it down and shooting behind. If you are naturally a quick shooter, fine – use that bit of extra time for these fundamentals. If you're not lightning fast, no matter; you might try just watching the birds that others shoot at and see for yourself how much time there really is – how long it takes a bird to fly those few unimportant feet.

You may have heard this a thousand times, but it's still worth repeating: Don't drop your gun the instant you fire whether you hit or miss. Keep it on your shoulder and your cheek firmly on the stock. If you have missed, you'll see where and why; if you've hit, you have a fine sight picture to store in your memory so you can repeat it next time. Follow-through is as important in shotgunning as it is in golf, tennis, or baseball.

You may not believe this, but even at the most extreme angles at trapshooting, the most you have to swing the muzzle is about a foot. In most field shooting, it's less. When you stop to think about that, it doesn't seem so hard, does it?

When you consider the small amount of time most of us have for our gunning and all the time and effort we put into our dogs and the money we spend on guns and this and that, it seems a little strange that so many don't extend themselves to learn to shoot a little better. That precious little time of a few seconds out of all the hours of planning and dreaming is the absolute culmination. I don't know about you, but I certainly wasn't born a good shot. Nor am I now by my standards, but I'm getting better because I know I have to work on it. I know I have to pick up a gun and dry fire a little during the week in my room. I have to think about it when I'm in the field. I have to remember and remind myself to pay attention to the fundamentals. And I promise that if it worked for me, it will work for anyone.

Recoil, Noise, and Flinching

Recoil is, without a doubt, the greatest enemy of the shotgunner. It makes you flinch; it makes you close both eyes; it makes you raise your head; in short – it hurts you and it hurts your shooting.

Basically a shotgun, to keep recoil at a minimum, should weigh about 96 times the amount of the shot charge. So if you shoot loads with 1¼ ounces of shot, your gun should not weigh less than about 7½ pounds. But suppose you're more sensitive than most to recoil – what then? And, for a variety of reasons, some guns just seem to kick more than others. What can you do about it? The first and simplest way is to add a little weight.

You can pack some shot, three or four ounces often does the trick, in the hollow of the stock under the recoil pad – make sure it's in tight or you'll end up with a harder kicker than you started out with! There are several commercial recoil reducers on the market that operate on a piston principle, weigh about eight ounces, and in my opinion work.

Recoil is often called "apparent recoil." In simple terms, an autoloader has the same recoil as any other gun that weighs the same; the automatic feeding system utilizes some of the recoil for chambering the next load and extraction, but more importantly it spreads the real recoil over a longer period of time – obviously softening the effect.

Holding on tighter with your left hand will help reduce recoil, but it probably will affect your shooting style – seems we can't have it both ways. Another cause of being hurt is the fact that many shotgun stocks have too much drop at the heel and comb or, as on many European guns, the comb is too sharp or too thin. If you build up the comb of your gun by using moleskin or by gluing a smooth piece of rubber or leather on the stock, it causes the gun to move back in a straighter line which means that you can more easily absorb the motion.

Butt ends of stocks are often very small in surface area. By putting on a large-surface recoil pad, you spread out the sting – and this can be very effective if you don't mind the looks. And of course, the most common easement of all is the recoil pad. A good one is a real help.

A beginning shooter is, unfortunately, the person who seems to get the most wallop. Why? Simple: He holds the gun too loose against the shoulder. The tighter you can pull the stock in with the trigger hand, within reason, the better off you'll be. Another simple answer, often overlooked by the field shooter, is to sew a recoil pad in the shoulder of your gunning jacket. A thin pad of foam rubber can work wonders. Just make sure you aren't going to end up with the stock too long after you do your padding. You don't need a lot, providing your padding also adds a little stiffness to the area, which "spreads out" the kick.

I'm convinced that a lot of the bothersome effect of recoil is the noise. There isn't much that the field shooter can do about that, but the clay target shooter can, and absolutely should, wear hearing protectors.

Now we come to the simplest device of all. Remember we talked about a gun weighing 96 times the amount of lead in the load? Well, why not reduce that – and that <u>really</u> works. A 1¼-ounce duck or pheasant load is not only much pleasanter to shoot than the heavier loadings, but it patterns better and will be a more effective long-range load than the bigger "magnums." It doesn't sound logical? Well, don't take my word for it – pattern a few of your favorite brands of 4's or 6's at 45 yards.

For your upland shooting, a light trap or skeet load, depending on the size of the bird and the cover you have to whack it through, will definitely do the job. By "light," as I said earlier, I mean the regular ounce or 1⅛ ounce, 2¾-dram load in a 12-bore gun. If I had to use just one upland load, I'd stick with the surprisingly effective light trap load using 7½ shot.

I don't particularly like the ultra-light shotgun – nor the idea of stuffing a near 12-gauge load in a 20-gauge gun. This makes the 20 a vicious little kicker and has spoiled gunning for many a lady and youngster who would have been much more comfortable shooting the same load in a 12 gauge.

If you have a special favorite shotgun and you've decided that the added recoil reducer isn't for you, you've put on a good recoil pad and the stock is nice and high – but the gun still punishes, there's one last resort, one that's quite effective in many cases. This is opening or "relieving" the forcing cone. It's a job that should be done by a competent gunsmith that specializes in such work; many of those who advertise their "custom choking" services are qualified to do this as well.

For every action, according to Sir Isaac Newton, there has to be an equal and opposite reaction: That's recoil – and that's one of the Laws of Motion. And it's still in effect – or was the last time I shot my shotgun.

Excessive recoil, if not controlled, can be a cause of a dread malady of experienced shooters: flinching. This is an affliction that I personally experience with great frequency – so much so that for many years all my competition guns have been fitted with release triggers – they work by pulling the trigger to set the sears and releasing the trigger to fire. They take a little getting used to but they've been a miracle device for me; of course, they are not for field use and belong only in the semi-isolation of competition games. But recoil isn't the only cause of flinching.

In an effort to reduce my flinching with the normal pull trigger – which I believe in many cases is caused by your brain not wanting a loud noise hurting your hearing – I use ear plugs whenever it's the least bit practical. I am handicapped, of course, by not being able to hear as well as I'd like, but those problems run in my family and I have never had "normal" hearing anyway.

Another solution, if that's the right word, came to me this past September while dove shooting in Mexico. The first two days I was shooting a short-barreled gun, one 26-inches long, and had a miserable time with my poor shooting from flinching. The third day I switched over to a 30-inch barrel and shot for several more days with little or no flinching simply because I had greatly reduced the volume of gunshot sound by moving it farther from my sensitive ears.

For those of us with the problem, the cures are few and not wholly effective in my experience, but the long barrel was a decided help. The real cure is not to let excessive hearing damage start in the first place, and now there's no excuse for it with the plenitude of ear protectors available. In my own case there were entirely too many shots fired from .45 pistols, machine guns, and trap and skeet guns with no protection whatsoever.

I know that many people are not affected by such noise – or think they're not. But hearing loss is insidious; it's there before you know it, and then it's too late.

Fortunately, extra barrels for the most common guns we use, the pumps and autoloaders, are not expensive. If the short gun you're using now is starting to hurt your hearing, don't wait to do something about it. Along with the comfort of shooting long barrels, you'll likely find that your shooting will improve overall. I know all the arguments about the quickness of short barrels and their ease of handling in heavy cover. But in the long run, you'll likely have a better average with the slightly heavier but smoother gun. They simply point and swing better for almost everyone.

Speed is only a positive function if everything else you do is in proportion! By that I mean your eyes must pick up and focus on the target quickly and you must establish your lead immediately as you quickly determine the target flight. Mess up on one thing, and all you've accomplished is a quick miss. Taking an extra second or so may seem less spectacular but as long as the results are what really count, you have to be the judge of whether you want to be fast or good – if you can't be both.

Another very common cause of flinching – infrequently spotted – is bad trigger pulls. If your gun doesn't hurt, your hearing isn't a problem, and you still flinch, have the pulls checked for travel and poundage and crispness. I like light, crisp triggers, about half the weight of the gun or slightly less. And don't forget that triggers have a way of mysteriously changing from season to season, affecting your shooting in maddening ways.

In sum, if you're flinching, try to determine the causes: recoil, noise, triggers, etc; or a combination of these. None of my suggestions will be totally effective, since flinching never seems to completely go away, but you will probably find some relief through personal experimentation. To use, badly, an old truism, it can't hurt.

Steel
Shot

I've shot more than a few geese and ducks using the
mandated steel shot, and it certainly has forced me to change a
couple of habits that I thought were ingrained. As you know,
the energy transference of the shot to the game is a great deal
of its lethality; assuming you have hit no vital parts nor broken
a wing, the shock effect of steel is much less than lead. Where I
used to (on my better days!) take one bird and then swing on
another, I find that with steel I virtually must always use a
second shot to anchor a bird, and often a third – regardless of
how "centered" the bird was with the first. Even so, I'm
finding birds sailing off to be retrieved dead; an easy thing
from some blinds, not so easy a thing from many others, using
a good retriever notwithstanding.

Steel shot is a light, solid projectile, frequently passing
through the bird with little apparent or immediate effect. You
might compare it to shooting a deer with a full metal jacket
bullet from a high velocity rifle. The bullet merely passes
through; providing it passes through vital tissue, lungs, heart,
or major arteries, you'll have your animal, but it's very unlikely
you'll drop it in its tracks.

There has been a lot of talk about altering or shortening your leads when using steel, but my experience has been that this is not worth the worry. For all practical purposes, at normal ranges you can point the gun just as you always did – you'll just have to pay attention for a little bit longer and be fully prepared to throw in a second or third shot to put the bird down.

This is one of the reasons for the recent introduction of loads made up of a mixture of heavy shot such as BBs with 2's or 4's. The BBs retain a high velocity and energy transfer while the smaller shot "fills in the holes." I shot a turkey last fall with one of these and was very impressed with the results and intend to use them on most of my waterfowl. This is not a cure-all, but it goes a long way in helping to overcome the weight-energy problems that are incumbent with steel shot. With the ordinary one-size steel shot, you will do yourself a big favor to pattern a few shells, using a choke no tighter than modified, and stay with the biggest shot size that patterns effectively. The only exception might be very small ducks that are usually shot at short ranges, teal or woodies for example. I found that steel 6's, close to the old lead size 7, were excellent since their pattern efficiency is very high. But don't try to stretch them past 40 yards.

I think that my days of enjoying high pass shooting are about over with steel shot, after having seen what happens to a 50-yard bird – or rather what doesn't happen right now. I admit that this isn't a great sacrifice, but it does narrow our range, and our ability to shoot well is restricted by the shells we are legislated to use.

None of this is a surprise to those of you who have kept up on the ballistics of steel, but I have always leaned in favor of field reports as opposed to those coming out of a test laboratory. Common sense leads me to believe that there will be an increase of lost birds that were perfectly pointed out until all of us learn to be more critical on our yardage and to either wait for or let go by a bird when we're in an area that makes long retrieves problematical. In effect, we now have a 45-yard governor built into our waterfowl shooting and if we have any conscience at all, we'd better learn how to judge it.

But it should be judged and learned for the sake of our waterfowl, not simply so that we won't "miss" so often. But that depends upon you.

Is shooting that well all that important? In my case, it used to be, but it isn't any more. I seem to get as much or more pleasure out of shooting well, but shooting less. I took very few woodcock last year because they were relatively difficult shots and if I missed – well, who cares? In the dove field I prefer the high, incoming shot because it's one that has always troubled me the most, and I can have a delightful shoot and end up with a handful of birds. I have always considered one or two ruffed grouse par or better for a day, and I don't have to find any reason for missing; grouse have always had my number and that suits me fine too. Otherwise, I'd have had fewer good reasons to keep fooling with "new" bird guns.

We ought to keep in mind that shooting is a game, a sport, and that there are rules, the very best kind – the ones that we privately bring according to our principles. I've been delighted to find on my excursions lately that more and more gunners may be going out as much as ever, but are very happily coming home with less in the hand and more in the heart.

The Driven Shoot

There's been a tremendous interest lately in shooting driven birds in Britain: how, when, and what – so I thought that perhaps you might like to know what it involves.

Right off I'm going to skip the driven grouse. First, there are only a very few good grouse moors in Britain, they are almost always booked years in advance, and they are both dreadfully expensive and totally unpredictable.

Most of us who go to Britain for driven birds mean pheasants – just like ours. The birds are put out in the "wild" on the estate, under the good care of a gamekeeper and his assistants, when they are poults – in mid-summer. They are usually kept in certain areas by feeding and vermin control and, except for being protected in this way, they are essentially wild – lean, strong flyers.

Although the pheasant season opens in October, the bulk of the shooting takes place from November through January when the weather is cool, the leaves have left the trees, and the probabilities of brisk winds are favorable. The traditional number for a shoot is eight "guns" (shooters), each of whom is given a number and that dictates his stand rotation throughout the day – this is an effort to ensure that everyone gets his chance at a hot corner.

The woods in most shooting estates are carefully maintained as bird covers, their size and location planned years ago so that the flight of the game can be controlled by the headkeeper according to the wind, and he then arranges the stand of guns accordingly. Of course, some covers are larger than others and the word quickly goes out that this or that drive is likely to be a big one – better bring an extra box or two of shells.

The beaters, usually locals who are paid a few dollars and fed lunch, always seem to deeply enjoy their part in the shoot. I've met beaters who are retired university professors, housewives, off-duty police officers – anyone and everyone who enjoys a good day of country walking with pay.

After the beaters are given their route and the guns are placed, the pickers-up, locals, and underkeepers with their dogs who will mark and retrieve the birds – and I'm always amazed that they almost never, ever miss one no matter how far it might sail away – are assembled and the drive begins.

On your stand you make note of your neighbors and plot out your own field of fire – both for safety and so as not to infringe on birds that are better shots for someone else. Of course, one thing is repeated over and over, and then over and over again – <u>no low shots</u>.

As the beaters come through the woods, you'll see hare or rabbits and a variety of birds come out. Most shoots forbid shooting at ground game in the interests of safety, but if a wood pigeon circles, you can feel free to take a shot. Most shooters use the traditional cartridge bag that holds about 100 shells; when the action gets furious, this is the simplest way to load your gun in a hurry.

An average day on a relatively modest shoot will see a bag of 200 to 250 birds from the eight guns. Many shoots will take many more birds, but I personally feel that 250 is enough shooting – enough to satisfy me, not too much where I get careless, and not too little where I lose interest.

The guns are predominantly 12 gauge side-by-side ejectors. At a few shoots where close to a thousand birds might be shot in a day, the shooters will need a pair of guns and a loader, but these are rare; one gun will see you through nicely. If a particular drive is known to be a heavy one, the shooter might have the aid of a "stuffer" – a person who stands beside him and stuffs fresh shells in his gun. This is just about as fast as using two guns – but the barrels can get a touch warm; I literally scorched a good pair of leather gloves on one drive when I used a stuffer. Now I carry a leather handguard and slip it over the barrels. The shells are a fraction more than an ounce of shot ($1\frac{1}{16}$), usually British 6's (our old 7) – very effective and very pleasant. They're also very cheap – about half what our shells sell for here.

The British "game choking" is commonly improved cylinder for the first barrel, and slightly tighter for the second. Skeet and skeet would do admirably. The beginner will often let birds fly by overhead that are well within the range of even a cylinder bore; it's a matter of watching the old hands – there are few birds on a drive that will ever exceed 35 or 40 yards. They just look like they're a hundred yards up; the British call them "archangels."

The cost of a shoot varies according to accommodations, which are frequently included in the package, but an ordinary shoot consists of 600-plus birds and room and board for four nights and three days. This is exclusive of air fare to the U.K. The birds themselves are a cash crop for the estate and are sold for restaurant use for two to three dollars each. But, all in all,

it's not a high-profit undertaking, and tradition and love of shooting still remain the greatest incentives.

Everyone always wants to know what to wear. The truth is that the Americans usually are more formally dressed than the British – but if you err, that's the right side. I wear a light wool shirt, necktie, and a Barbour-type coat.

Almost everyone wears the plus-two trousers – what you used to call knickers. (What the British call knickers are ladies' underwear.) High stockings and a good sturdy, low-top boot – the little L.L. Bean leather-top rubbers are perfect. The plus-twos are by no means mandatory; any light wool trouser is fine as long as you don't mind getting them muddy. The British wear a knee-high rubber boot ("Wellies") and they're fine and inexpensive over there. You just have to realize that the place is narrow from sea to sea and the chances of rain are close to 100% – the plus-twos don't get wet and sopping like long pants do, and they're easier to walk in. The British are very practical about dress, as unusual as it looks to us. I don't know what they'd say about our blaze orange and red-and-black buffalo plaids, either – but you'll be very comfortable doing it their way over there.

If you have an idea about trying this sort of shooting, which I enthusiastically endorse, I suggest you gather the whole group, eight guns, and then book your trip. One or two guns are hard to place in a shoot, and it's a lot more fun being with your own friends.

The
Traveling
Wingshooter

A few years ago, I had my "shooting bag" stolen from the trunk of my car. In it was a rather miscellaneous collection of a few extra gun parts, a couple of screwdrivers, two pairs of shooting glasses, and some other odds and ends. It wasn't until I tried to get some return from my insurance company that the full value of what I had lost occurred to me along with the idea of every so often making a list of some things I had and their value.

I suggest that you take an hour or so off and list your guns on two 3 x 5 file cards: make, gauge, serial number, and any distinguishing features – engraving, vent ribs, etc. Note when and from whom you got it, what it cost then, and what it would cost to replace it now. Cameras, binoculars, good knives, and other such stuff should be listed as well. Keep one set of cards around and update as necessary and the other set in a separate place – ideally a safe deposit box. I've known of some trying times that people have had when their stuff got stolen or lost in a fire or just lost – as can too easily happen on an airline. I automatically insure my guns for a couple of thousand on every flight just in case they get misplaced or, as often happens, broken.

It wouldn't hurt to photograph any especially good stuff you might have. I know of one case where a fine English double was stolen and later recovered by the police when they arrested a man using the gun in a holdup. The police insisted that they needed the gun "as evidence" and then put the original owner through a real mess trying to prove that the gun was his in the first place. It took well over a year and the help of an attorney for the man to finally get his gun back. And don't think that your insurance company is terribly softhearted when it comes to taking your word that your Boss or Purdey or Parker was stolen from your car or your motel room.

The least expensive regular gun insurance that I know of, by the way, is that offered to the members of the National Rifle Association. Your home insurance coverage will often help out as well, but don't wait until you have to try to collect to find out. Do it now!

It is illegal to travel on an airline with a gun unless it is declared and examined. If you put it in your duffel bag and just check it through as baggage and it's lost or damaged, you're out of luck. Don't forget to keep a set of keys to your gun case where they're handy or you'll be sorting through a pile of stuff and looking in pants pockets as I had to do last year returning from a Western duck hunt.

My own traveling gun cases are now heavy aluminum. I say "now" because it took two broken fiberglass cases and a damaged gun to get my attention. The important feature in a good gun case, other than solid construction, is strong lock hasps that are firmly riveted to the case – and the more the better. When you get one, paint your name and address on the case or have it engraved on a plate and rivet that to the case.

The usual name tags or airline stickers won't take enough rough handling.

One more bit of often-forgotten advice about travel, and that's to try to take enough of your favorite ammunition with you. You won't believe the number of country stores that don't carry shells at all any more or those that won't have 16 or 28 gauge in any shot size, and there are plenty that won't have light 8's or 9's or even 7½'s. Make sure before you go, if you can, or bring your own. And don't put them in the gun case with your shotgun – that's also illegal.

If you take extended trips in remote country, you ought to get in the habit of bringing a few spare parts along with you – firing pins and major springs – and learn how to replace them and have a couple of small screwdrivers along to do the job. Chances are you'll never need them, but I've seen it happen. Once is enough – when it's your gun. Don't ever expect anyone to have anything that you'll need – the old and true theory is that if you don't have it when you need it, it might as well not exist.

You're not apt to be too far from civilization when you're bird hunting, but experience has proven that when things go wrong, they go at the worst possible time and in the worst possible place. I no longer go anywhere without a bottle of a broad-spectrum antibiotic like Amphicillin or Tetracycline and a strong pain reliever like Percodan in my shaving kit. I have had to use both. If you have any special needs, I assume that you plan in advance for emergency happenings. And if you do any traveling out of the country, be sure you have a copy of your prescription with you. Our faithful Customs Service can take some very odd attitudes with certain medications.

One of the most helpful ideas I can give you about traveling is to make a list of everything – even socks, underwear, and alarm clock. Before you pack it up, lay it all out on the bed and go through the list like an airline pre-flight check. I know this sounds silly, but believe me, you'll end up in Mexico without a visa or in Hudson's Bay without long underwear at least once. I travel quite a bit and am now keeping a notebook that involves a variety of climates. It's too simple to forget bug repellent when it's snowing at home where you're packing. You may learn the hard way that most of Scotland is about the same latitude as Labrador, and that in a lot of Canada and our Northwest it can snow pretty heavily in September.

Traveling plans don't restrict themselves only to the exotic places. You have to learn that anywhere that isn't home is in some way "foreign." I've been in duck camps an easy day's drive from where I live and found them with fewer amenities (such as soap, towels, and toilet paper) than you might expect in the "real back of beyond." I don't believe in being uncomfortable or unclean unless there's no choice; I don't believe that roughing it a little means going without sleep or decent food. Being exhausted or physically hurting beyond reason isn't showing how tough you are – it's stupid.

The smart traveler takes good care of his equipment and himself; the best insurance is your common sense, in most cases. Before the season opens or you are about ready to leave for somewhere, you should have taken a look at your hip boots and your rainwear, remembered where you left your hat and gloves, checked your shell supply, and looked for your dog whistle and the lead.

I probably really couldn't and I wouldn't bet a whole lot on it, but I could come pretty close to packing for almost anywhere in a few hours. But, as I readily admit, I had to learn the hard way. You might do me a favor, however, if you find where I left that little two-cup Thermos, let me know. I can't seem to find mine anywhere, and I'm kind of hoping it's right next to that little flashlight I absolutely never go anywhere without.

No doubt that a lot of the fun of traveling is the anticipation and the getting ready, the sorting of gear, and checking it over. But the real icing on the cake is when you know after you get there that you had it just right – at least this once.

Just What
Is A
Good Shot?

One of the facts of our modern times is that few shotgunners will ever experience the number of birds our forefathers did. Consequently, the learning process required for becoming a "good" shot either has to be polished on the clay target ranges or by simply going out more – especially for the large bag limit birds such as doves. I've long preached that the ideal solution to becoming a good shot is having a couple of cases of shotshells run through your shotgun. Not that it's such a practical or easy method. It's a fact of life; the more you shoot, the better you'll get. Like golf, not as much as we'd like can be learned from reading. Not surprising either is the fact that many of our truly fine shots can't give you a reasonable enlightening of just how they put it all together.

Of course, being a good shot should and ought to vary a little. Today's scores on the skeet and trap fields are almost incredible. Five-hundred straights, under the rigors of first-class competition, are commonplace.

A good day's shooting in a duck blind with a 45 mile-an-hour wind and spooky birds might be one bird out of every three or four shots. When they're pitching into the decoys, you ought to do twice as well. Cover is a great factor in upland gunning as well as weather again. And there are days of mysterious influences when the birds just fly harder and faster and sooner – or something.

I am fond of the occasional day in the live pigeon ring where I believe the finest shooting anywhere is to be seen. In the course of a 100-bird match, the winning score should be around 95 or 96. There are very few 100 straights – not that several shooters won't kill that many. But, remember that in the pigeon ring the fence is only 15 yards from the traps. It's about 20 inches high and the gunner is often standing as far as 34 or even 35 yards back from the traps. Many is the perfectly centered and often dead bird that falls over the boundary. You need to be a superb shot and have a heavy dash of luck too, now and then. During a year of competition, shooting at several hundred birds, a fine live pigeon average is anything around 88 to 90 percent. Unfortunately, a lot of us who enjoy this sort of competition fall into that ticklish category of being "too good to quit and not good enough to win."

I've been a big advocate of not keeping score in field shooting. I don't see the point of it, except for curiosity – fine for those who like to maintain a private and personal record but not in the competitive sense. I have, for quite a few years, spent a little time in England or Scotland each year shooting driven birds – grouse, pheasant, and partridge when there were any. Since we're buying our shells from the shooting estate, a pretty close accounting is kept and it's been a tradition there, for several reasons, to keep a good estimate of shots fired and birds taken. So now we come to a nice point: <u>Just what is a good shot?</u> Well, I've got some records of people I know and who, in my opinion, are good. They shoot a lot, and their guns are first grade and fitted to them with a great deal of care, knowledge, and experience.

Their personal records in dove shooting, which they do a lot of, run about 60 percent in an average year of more than 500 birds. (They shoot in several different countries, in case you're worried.) In their records of all shooters, they believe that one dove for five shells is about average. They feel that the average duck gunner, to consider himself good, ought to take at least two ducks for five shots. Most don't do that well. An excellent gun will average a bit over 60 percent on waterfowl. A good quail shot should take two birds with three shells; a first-class shot will average around 70 percent.

In British driven pheasant shoots, they consider a good shot will average one bird with three cartridges. An excellent shot will do about twice as well – averaging over 70 percent.

Now let's look a little closer at a first-class shot; not a hypothetical compound, but a person I often shoot with. His dove guns are 12 gauge and custom choked for his favorite brand of number 8 shot. He likes a fairly tight boring because he usually lets his friends shoot first and has to work on what gets by. He chooses to take the more difficult shots to keep in training, so to speak. He is a student of the game of shooting and works at it constantly, as would a low-handicap golfer or fine tennis player. His quail guns and duck guns and pheasant guns are likewise rather specialized. For quail he prefers a 28 gauge – a gun he will use for doves as well in certain situations. His gun for driven pheasant, almost all of which are high and fast-climbing incomers offering little time to "get ready," is the traditional 12 bore, quite straight stocked, a bit longer in length of pull than our walk-up guns, and bored to shoot about 35-40 percent in both barrels. The typical English load is, by the way, an ounce of 6's – the equivalent of our old 7's – and if you put it in the right place, it will do the job perfectly.

I hope I haven't painted a picture of a rich and eccentric shooter, since that's far from the case. He's just an ordinary working man who has focused his available time around shotgunning and put a great deal of thought and effort as well as practice into it. Like anyone who gets a chance to shoot a variety of birds, he's learned that the old "one gun" thing is nonsense. My live pigeon gun is almost <u>never</u> used for anything else. It's not good for anything else. It's too often not good at pigeons either, but that is the usual case of the steerer not doing what he's supposed to. If I shoot a round of skeet or trap with my pigeon gun, it's only an effort to tune up my gun handling for pigeons, never with any idea of breaking a decent score on clay targets; the gun is much too fast for trap and much too tightly bored for skeet.

So, as usual when we sneak a look at the bottom line, we find that the better-than-average person — be he engaged in golf, gunning, whatever — has deeper-than-average dedication, better-than-average equipment, and does more-than-an-average amount of it. He works at it.

A well-off doctor (I know that's redundant) has been asking me to help him with his trap shooting. Because he uses a duck gun with a field stock, I've refused, telling him that he has to get a trap gun or forget shooting good scores. He finally did break down and after two rounds went from shooting less than 15 to breaking over 20. He was just stubborn or skeptical or one of the too many who believe that if you're good you can shoot anything. Well, that's true. But you won't shoot anything well.

Another friend that I occasionally gun with is, in my opinion, a truly great shot. Not ordinary great either, <u>great</u> great. Last fall he happened to show up at a duck camp where I was, just to say hello, and was invited to shoot. He hadn't brought one of his own guns and accepted the loan of an

870 Remington pump. Where you or I would have probably just taken it out and let it go at that, he produced a roll of electrician's tape, rummaged around and found some cardboard, and in about five minutes had the gun to where it fitted him fairly well – the way he liked a duck gun to fit. To say that he shot it well would be like saying da Vinci knew how to draw. No doubt he could have done very well with the gun as it was – but why let such a little bit of effort stand in the way of doing better? It's an attitude we can learn something from.

For those of us who don't shoot a lot, the attitude is often "the hell with it." Funny that we should be that way when we're the ones who need all the help we can get. I wonder if any of his fellow pros ever needled Jack Nicklaus about being too fussy about his clubs. Oh, I know they needled me, but that's different. And I am very, very sorry to have to admit it. The only private consolation I have is the knowledge of how I'd shoot if I weren't more than a little fussy about what gun I'm shooting.

ODDS
&
ENDS

T his little section could best be called "Odds & Ends," I guess, because there isn't anything here really earth-shattering, just things I wanted to talk about with you – quick notes from my notebook that will hopefully make your gunning a little more pleasant and your days afield a little brighter.

Just what should you see when you look over a gun barrel? If you place your cheek snugly against the stock and your ribbed gun has a middle and front bead, the sights should stack like a figure 8. If you shoot a plain-barreled gun, you should see three or four inches of gun barrel just behind the front sight – and see <u>none</u> of the receiver whatsoever.

Suppose you don't. If you see more of the barrel or rib than what I've described, your gun is shooting a bit high. If you're successful with it, leave it alone. If it's kicking your cheekbone or bruising your face, take off a <u>shade</u> (which I believe is about a light eighth of an inch), and work in this increment until you've got it comfortable. If you're a right-handed shooter, you could also take another eighth off the <u>inside</u> of the comb where it touches your cheek, but go easy.

If you're going to add a recoil pad to a shotgun, I suggest that you have the gunsmith check the pitch. Most factory stocks are built with a bit of down pitch which can make for a low-shooting gun. I have all mine recut to have 0 degrees of pitch. Pitch is the angle at which the stock is cut off at the butt.

Without the formalities of patterning, a good check is to

throw your gun up quickly and shoot at a leaf or stick in a pond or stream and see where the shot hits. Another is to make sure you keep your head on the stock and re-check your target after a miss to find where your first shot was. I really believe that as many are missed by being low as having insufficient lead.

•   •   •   •   •   •

In trapshooting, as you might know, a lot of shooters have the barrels bent upward a bit, but this is chancy as it involves trial and error – in my case, mostly error. But for years I shot a Model 21 Winchester with bent barrels and achieved pretty fair results.

They used to say that "to hit is history, to miss is mystery." No reason for that to be so. Experiment a little. It can't hurt. Ideally, I think a shotgun pattern should be about 60/40 in pattern percentage – that is, 60 percent of the pattern above a point of aim when you pattern by "bench-resting." When you do pattern for height, do it at only 20 yards; it will be much easier to determine any vagaries.

The most risky way to regulate barrels is to have the chokes made a little eccentric to throw the shot charge higher. The phrase "good gunsmith" should come into your mind. If all this sounds a bit picky, remember how little we get to go out for the most part and how discouraging it is to lose the too few fair chances we <u>do</u> have. If a few minutes of trial with a favorite gun can change your average, why not try it? I don't know about you, but I need all the help I can get.

•   •   •   •   •   •

If your gun has a vent rib, take a little extra time to check under it for rust spots and clean out the bridges with an oiled pipe cleaner regularly.

Some gunners, especially those who do a lot of

waterfowling, like to coat the outside metal with a hard wax, the stuff you'd put on your car. I haven't tried it, but I don't see why it wouldn't be a good idea – providing you remember to touch it up every so often. I have been using a good hard furniture wax on my gunstocks for years, and find that one light coating seems to help avoid a lot of scratches. I use the same wax on my good leather gun cases for the same reason.

●　　　●　　　●　　　●　　　●　　　●

If your leather case is lined with felt, toss in a couple of mothballs when you store it for any length of time, but don't keep a gun in one; as a storage place, it tends to collect moisture.

I've learned the hard way to buy good stuff and then make some effort to take care of it. And when I look at what's happened to prices, I go right back and wax and polish it all one more time. That way, when I lose something, as I inevitably will, it will be found in good shape!

●　　　●　　　●　　　●　　　●　　　●

One of my meticulous friends who is paranoid about having a light gun carries a belt knife, two boxes of shells, a flask, a flashlight, and enough other needless impedimenta in his hunting coat to break down a mule. I don't see the sense in spending a fortune for a six-pound 12 gauge gun, and carrying 10 pounds of odds and ends in your pockets.

●　　　●　　　●　　　●　　　●　　　●

Ever wonder about the American chokes compared with the British system? Here they are:

American	British	Percentage at 40 yards
Cylinder	Cylinder	40%
Imp. Cylinder	Quarter Choke	50%
Modified	Half Choke	60%
Imp. Modified	Three Quarter	65%
Full	Full	70%

• • • • • •

What do you do when your autoloader sometimes doesn't work? I have to assume that you followed the instructions for cleaning it every hundred rounds or so (and you haven't over-oiled the working parts). I also assume that you don't make the same mistake I have – and you've followed the little diagram that tells you how to put the rings, etc., back in the right order.

Okay. You've done all that, but every once in a while the gun doesn't eject the empty, and there you are, hung up in the middle of your only chance at a pure double on grouse all year. You use some very colorful language to ask, "What happened?"

If you move the gun <u>forward</u> just at the time the recoil mechanism begins its ejection cycle, you can sometimes effectively dampen the action enough to cause a "malfunction."

Just try to hang on a little tighter and you'll quit having that kind of hang-up – and who knows, you might even keep your head on the gun where it belongs so you can talk about having "a pair dead in the air" more than once or twice a season.

• • • • • •

"Cast-off" is the angle at which the barrels are set in relation to the stock. The barrels are to the left of the stock for a right-hand shooter (cast-off) and the reverse for a left-hand shooter (cast-on). The toe, or bottom, of the stock is also angled to conform to the shooter's anatomy.

I think I shoot better with a bit of cast. (It lines the gun barrel up better, straight under my master eye.) And I know it's more comfortable, because the slight angle on the gun butt now closely conforms to the strange curves of my chest-and-shoulder area.

I think this might be an especially nifty thing for a lady shooter to try – if she doesn't mind having the gun looking a little funny in order to have it feel a lot more comfortable. To try some toe-out, drill a second hole about ⅜ inch to the right of the bottom (or if you're a lefty, the other way around) screw holding your recoil pad, and replace the pad. Give it a good try, and see if it doesn't feel better and point better. If not, go back to where you were – nothing ventured, nothing gained.

If you feel the sharp edge of the inside pad, take a file to it and smooth the rubber with a little emery. I do this on all my recoil pads anyway.

This bit of toeing out of the recoil pad, especially on my trap guns, also helps me mount the gun in the same place instead of moving it around and giving me another "inexplicable" miss. I know it's not a true cast-off, but it helps me.

●　　　●　　　●　　　●　　　●　　　●

One of shotgunning's favorite arguments is this: Are you better off with a pattern that's dense with small shot, or a less tight pattern with larger shot that holds a greater energy potential?

In general, the consensus is in favor of multiple hits with smaller shot because of the increased shock effect, and the fact that large shot and decent patterns rely heavily on the efficiency of the choke and the quality of the shells themselves and their uniformity. But, as we all know, some guns don't obey the laws. They, for a lot of known and unknown reasons, will shoot one brand or one shot size a lot better than anything else.

The trouble with this is obvious: Unless we spend a near-absurd amount of time and money patterning, we never will know if one special shell will make all that much of an improvement. But you could do it with 8's for example, if you use that shot size for quail hunting. Or you could pick a load of 4's or 2's that agreed with your favorite duck gun. For the same reason, your top tournament skeet and trap shooters have a favorite brand.

I'm shifting away from the "pattern vs. penetration" argument itself – what you need to know is what works in your gun, for your game, at the yardages you usually shoot. What difference will it make – really? That's hard to say, but it should make enough to make some testing worthwhile. You'll find some shells seem to kick more than others. You'll find that the harder the shot (the more antimony mixed in with the lead), the better your patterns and penetration will be. Unhappily for us, however, shotshell manufacturers use a shorthand of their own design and don't tell us much more than "Max.Load #6 Shot" or a dram-equivalent measure that doesn't have much real meaning either.

I know that one brand of 7½ trap loads patterns better than the others in my over-under. Significantly? No, not all that critical, but it also seems to be a little easier to shoot – and the combination gives me a lot of confidence in that particular shell.

I once experimented with a fairly expensive imported nickel shotshell that not only loosened my fillings, but didn't pattern in my gun at all well. Yet this same shell is the most popular in the European live-pigeon circuit. It sure shoots well in a lot of guns – but not mine.

And if, in this imperfect world, I erred – I'd err on the side of having fairly well-choked guns and patterns that were a shade on the tight side. A minority voice, I know – but that's my vote.

Most of the time when we miss, we blame ourselves. And most of the time we're right – but not always.

When I talk to a shooter, after a consistent series of misses, about the possibility of his gun barrel being crooked, he usually smiles and marks me down as a crank.

Well, let me tell you of just a few who didn't. One is an Olympic hopeful who had a lot of misses at trap on left-angling birds. I suggested he bench-rest and pattern his gun. Guess what? The upper-left quarter of the pattern was virtually blank, and the bulk of the load was in the right half. Fifteen minutes with a gunsmith and that problem was solved.

Another friend was breaking every target – of those that he broke at all – on the left side. Both barrels of his over-under, when properly patterned, were a full ⅔ of a pattern width off to the left.

How many second barrels that gunners get for their pumps and autos shoot in the same place as the original barrel? Virtually none – if you want to be exact. And if you want good trap or skeet scores – or consistent results on birds – you want a barrel to shoot where it should – exactly.

A gun barrel is a lot more fragile than most people believe. A careless toss into a car trunk or someone knocking it out of a rack at a shoot can bend it or take the barrel out of round, creating eccentric pattern placement. I've asked several prominent choke experts how many barrels they got to work on that shot where they should. The answer? Very, very few.

Any competent gunsmith can bring the barrel back to shooting where it should, either by straightening it out if it's bent or getting the muzzle back in round if that's what's wrong.

A large part of good shooting is confidence in your shotgun – and this is an easy way to solve a problem that's a lot more prevalent than most gunners will believe…until they bench-rest it for pattern.

• • • • • •

For bird hunting, I wear a glove on my left hand to fight brush and briars – I didn't see any sense in buying a pair since I only needed one, so I got onto golf gloves; they're light and flexible, not too expensive, and they are easy to clean.

• • • • • •

Even though I don't normally wear glasses, I do when I go gunning – everywhere except in the duck blind, because they reflect light and I can't yet keep my head still and down the way I should. I like the lightly tinted grey lens to cut a little of the glare, but basically I keep them on to protect my eyes from snapping twigs. I have had too many close calls and know too many shooters who have had worse. I keep a pair of the photometric type (the ones that change density according to the light conditions) in my clay target kit because of the stuff floating around in the air – powder residue, dust, and the like.

• • • • • •

If you rummage through my hunting coat, you'd be likely to find a little piece of electrician's tape (I've never had to use it, but it's a habit), a piece of rope (I use it a lot), a throw-away flashlight (always in my duck coat for pre-dawn stumbling), and a couple of Band-Aids. (I try to remember to carry an extra dog whistle and a pocket knife but don't average better than 50%.) My Swiss Army knife, in a belt pouch, serves for any tools I feel I might need.

• • • • • •

I once was pretending to admire a friend's heirloom Model 21 Winchester. It had been a lovely gun a very long time ago,

beautifully figured walnut stock, 28-inch barrels bored modified and full, a straight hand English grip, and nice accessories all in a fitted leather case. The gun hadn't really been abused, it was just that he'd never taken care of it. The barrels were slightly pitted outside from a film of rust. The ejectors were gummed up, rust spots covered the trigger, guard, and receiver, and the stock and forend were scratched and dull from coats of poorly applied oil and varnish. The recoil pad was half rotten, and the leather case, a treasure in itself, was filthy and badly scuffed.

He said that he guessed he ought to take a little better care of it, but "one of these days" he intended to give it to a gunsmith for a good cleaning.

Of course, the gun was long past anything a "good cleaning" might have accomplished. It should have had a good cleaning every year for the past five years that he'd had it. And he could have done most of it himself – in about 10 minutes.

Your "good" gun doesn't have to wear the label of a famous London maker to be worth a lot more than you might guess. But whatever it's worth in dollars, it's certainly worth a little time and thought to keeping it as good as it is or perhaps making it a little better.

The general outside condition of a gun is a fairly obvious situation. But if I were sending a quality gun to any good gunsmith for a general overhaul, I'd also have him make an extra set of firing pins and the critical springs. In a few years it might be near impossible, and certainly extremely expensive, to have these simple items made – and they do break. And while I was at it, especially if dealing with a sidelock gun, I'd have a couple of screwdrivers made to exactly fit the engraved screws. It's a lot cheaper than replacing broken screws or having them re-engraved.

I was shooting pheasant in England last year, and one of the party had an exquisite Boss sidelock that was giving him trouble. He'd just had it restocked in Portugal by "a famous stockmaker." The work was terrible, and I suspected that there was a loose splinter or something simple that had gone wrong and asked him if he had the gun's turnscrews, as the English call them. He said he didn't, but he had a screwdriver in the kit of his car. I told him if <u>he</u> wanted to take the locks off, I'd look at the gun, but it was his decision. He finally rummaged around and came up with the kind of screwdriver that comes on a key ring. He took the locks off, ruining the screws, but we did get the junk out and had him back shooting in short order. The moral is that a good, fitted screwdriver is cheap and often indispensable.

●   ●   ●   ●   ●   ●

While we're on the subject, remember that accessories aren't any good if you don't have them with you. Get yourself a small needle-plunger oiler (the kind that looks a little like a fountain pen), a tube of good gun grease, and a spray can of water-displacing protectant like WD-40. It's best to have a gunsmith show you where to put the <u>one or two</u> drops of oil and where the bearing surfaces need a dab of grease. Try your best to keep any of this stuff off the stock wood. I store my guns lying down, with the receivers up so that oil doesn't seep into the wood. Oil not only discolors, but will badly soften the wood fibers. I'm not that fussy about polishing the bores, but it can't hurt, followed by a light spray of WD-40 (inside and out) or some similar protectant if the gun has been wet or will be stored for a while.

If your gun needs a new recoil pad, I like the looks of the solid-style pads. Any gunsmith should have them, and while you're having it replaced, put a little good wax over the open-end grain of the stock – again, it can't hurt.

Among the many advantages of having this kind of work done in the winter or spring is that you won't be rushing your craftsman and he'll have the time to do the extra niceties like tuning the ejectors, checking various places for fit and wear, and making the parts or finding them that you'll need. If you postpone this until just before the shooting season, you'll likely get just what you can in the little time you've allowed him to do your work.

As with anything, get an estimate; if it seems high, ask about it. Most good gunsmiths are scrupulously honest, but some are absolute perfectionists and will insist on re-doing it their way. If it's been some time since you had any work done, be prepared for a shock.

Even if you don't need upgrading or any major work, it's great insurance to have a good gun taken apart and cleaned a minimum of once every two or three years. Little specks of rust, cracked screws, or springs are better fixed and checked now than fumed over in the middle of the bird season when your old favorite breaks down. In my fussy turn of mind, there aren't many men I want working on a couple of my guns. I've seen too many good guns severely damaged, or in a few cases ruined, by amateurs. One that I recall was a friend's Model 21 20 gauge that he gave to someone to reblue. The so-called gunsmith removed the old bluing with a wire wheel and the touch of a blacksmith – leaving the gun with deeply scratched and scored barrels that definitely took it a long way from the status it deserved.

Do not send a gun before you talk or correspond with your gunsmith. Tell him what you think the gun needs and get an estimate – but be ready to hear that he suggests or insists that this or that be done for your satisfaction. All guns should be shipped insured for as close to their replacement value as you can manage.

• • • • • •

Over the years of shooting, I've accumulated a closet full of clothes supposedly designed to keep you dry, warm, safe from the dreaded briar and thorn, and not only make you look younger and thinner, but help you shoot faster and straighter. These feature exotic fabrics, designs that are the envy of engineers, and enough belts and straps and pockets to strike envy into the heart of a Green Beret.

But if you see me shooting skeet or trap, I'll be the guy wearing a sort of old and nondescript sweater, maybe with a leather patch sewn on the shoulder.

My field outfits have been narrowed down the same way, through years of experimentation in the search for comfort and practicality; stuff that's as easy to pack and keep clean as it is functional. I haven't worn a so-called "hunting coat" in years, nor do I much care for the "faced" hunting pants. Both garments are too restrictive; you can't really stretch out in a hunting coat, and the pants are almost guaranteed to be too heavy and too hard to walk in, especially in the kind of cover that requires a lot of leg-lifting – like bogs or blowdowns.

I hate to have a garment that restricts my arm movements; I don't like a lot of weight hanging on my shoulders – it's just too confining and tiring. So I long ago went to a sort of vest – really only a pocket for shells and the usual junk we lug around. I like the idea of being able to wear a choice of shirts or sweaters under practically nothing; it's easy to add or subtract as the temperature changes.

But I've finally come to something I like even better for bird hunting: just a belt with three pockets on it – the rig that is usually called a "dove belt." I use one pocket for shells, one for glasses, gloves, chewing tobacco, and incidentals, and the one in the rear is more than ample for the few birds I'll take in an ordinary day. Since I'm the forgetful type, I keep a small knife on the belt permanently and have added a clip in case I want to carry a dog lead or flushing whip.

These arrangements are inexpensive, extremely comfortable, easy to clean, and easy to pack for travel. I'm just a little ashamed that it took me so long to discover the thing.

Over my shirt or sweater I have a broad choice. On wet or cool days, I wear a jacket like the British Barbour coat or an insulated outfit if it's really chilly. But usually I'm out there in an old sweater or chamois shirt and with the almost-mandatory blaze orange hat so none of my hunting friends will mistake me for a quail or woodcock.

Lately, I've come to like a really roomy jacket – one of the few I can shoot in comfortably – called the Hogg's lightweight, made in Scotland. I favor the Hill mode, naturally, although I believe the nomenclature is based on topography rather than an aging writer of the same name. I wear the jacket as a dress coat when I travel – you see this same sort of coat by the thousands in London or New York – the rare incidence of fashion and common sense joining hands.

Another of the great discoveries for me was the urethane chap. I just pull a pair of these on (they're really leggings) over khaki pants or blue jeans, and off I go. The chaps weigh next to nothing and are quite wetproof and windproof without being too warm. They're slippery and let your knees slide under them for real ease of walking anywhere. When the hunt is over or you stop in a diner for lunch, you just slide them off and you're as presentable as you'll ever be (at least I am). Again, they're easy to clean and don't take up any more packing room than a pair of heavy socks. Chaps in a bit heavier material are also offered for those of us who have a deep and permanent respect for rattlers and the like – a position where I am second to none!

My favorite footwear is still the old Bean boot, but I have

grown fond of lightweight all-leather boots as well. I have long given up looking good for feeling good, and now that I can do it with a minimum of fuss and bother, I'm not about to be lured away.

·   ·   ·   ·   ·   ·

I have long wished that hunters – all of us – would give a little more thought to our public image.

Next time you walk into a diner during the shooting season and you see your counterpart wearing his plastic orange cap, a coat stiff with old blood stains, and sporting a belt knife that would be more at home on a sugar plantation, think about how this looks to the people who don't hunt. If you were a farmer, who do you want hunting on your land? What sort of spokesman do you want when the locals start complaining about shotgun patterns on all the road signs, and the newspapers carry the traditional story about the pet dog or cow or even horse that was gunned down?

We all talk about "ethics." But the simple effort of putting our best face to the public seems to have been overlooked. I somewhat resent having to wear a license the size of a wanted poster, and I have mixed feelings about being draped in hunter orange; an incarcerated felon looks like a banker by comparison. I'm ashamed that our elected officials don't trust us not to steal game or shoot each other – but whose fault is it?

Looking a little better won't solve the problem – but it won't hurt you or our image. And after you've thought about it for a long time, tell me why a person out for an afternoon in a bird cover has to wear more camouflage than a combat infantryman. Maybe it's time we all grew up before it's too late.

·   ·   ·   ·   ·   ·

There are a few things I do to my duck guns that might interest you. First, I put on a recoil pad if it doesn't already have one. This keeps the stock from slipping down in the shoulder, and any softening of the kick is always welcome. If you don't want to go to the expense of having one fitted, fine. Get one that's a little bigger and just screw it on. It won't look as good, but it will be even more comfortable.

I also prefer a stock closer to <u>trap</u> dimensions than <u>field</u>. If you can't order a gun with this higher stock, a little moleskin from the drugstore placed on the comb does the same thing. This makes the gun shoot a little higher, meaning that wherever the bird goes, you can see it over your gun barrel and still have it in the center of the pattern. It may take a little getting used to, but in the long run you'll come to appreciate it, especially on those ducks that suddenly seem to drop low as they're coming in.

I've shot everything as a duck gun: autos, over-unders, side-by-sides, and pumps. The over-unders are hard to load in a duck blind and, like the side-by-sides, getting a little too valuable to drag around in the marsh or rattle around in a duck boat. The autos are fine if you take care of them, but if I only had one gun to go ducking with, it would have to be the pump. I like the way they point, I like the ease of loading and unloading, and they work almost no matter what.

Again my personal opinion, but I think duck shooting, taking them as they come, is the most difficult wingshooting. A box of light trap loads run through your gun at a session with the hand trap, or a couple of rounds of trap at the gun club with the old duck gun makes a lot of sense. Just having your duck gun out where you can pick it up and throw it to your shoulder a few minutes a day before the season is a good way to wake up some of the muscles and get used to putting your gun in the right place on your shoulder. Your wife and kids probably think you're a little crazy anyway, so what's the harm?

I'd like to make one more suggestion: The people I hunt

with often take turns in the blind. Not just the man on the right taking his bird – he is the only one that shoots <u>at all</u>. In the long run, we all get the same amount of shooting and we feel better about doing it this way. And, it's easier on the dogs and their marking, which makes <u>everybody</u> happy.

There are in our society many, many ways to impoverishment. All to the good, for it means that we who own too many guns, too many dogs, spend too much time frittering with duck boats, blinds, and their own individual impedimenta are most often unnoticed by our self-important neighbors. Fine. We have our secret vices to ourselves beginning at four o'clock in the morning as we labor quietly over pancakes and sausage and a couple of eggs over-easy, with the extra going to the black or yellow or golden dog waiting, not too patiently, by the hip boots and the gun case in the kitchen corner.

Our days that are spent in our mysterious comings and goings in the dark are for our own amusement; mostly private times, telling our hopes and fears to our dog who listens with patience and understanding; fooling with duck calls, moving a decoy a foot here or a yard there, and discussing with mock seriousness the advantages of a couple of thousandths of an inch in choke boring or the size of a piece of shot. The mixed emotions that come with the fallen birds are unexplainable, except between you and me, and almost never require words.

It's an ancient, honorable, and somewhat mysterious occupation to be, at once, both protector and taker of these birds. I'm not quite sure I completely understand it, which is just as well, but I do know that I have to be there every so often to replenish something in me. I'm not sure just what it is, but I know when it's done and done right.

I know you understand exactly what I'm talking about. But then, only another shotgunner would.

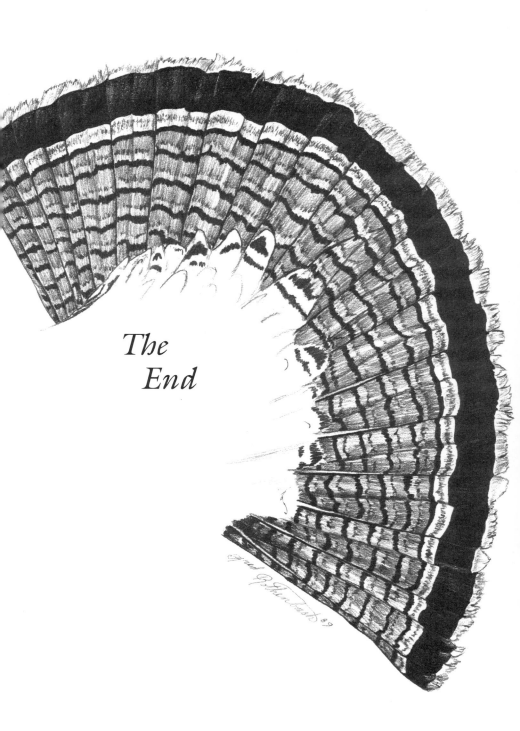

*The
End*